LIFE WITHOUT BREAD

Life Without Bread

How a Low-Carbohydrate Diet Can Save Your Life

Christian B. Allan, Ph.D.
and
Wolfgang Lutz, M.D.

KEATS PUBLISHING

LOS ANGELES

NTC/Contemporary Publishing Group

Library of Congress Cataloging-in-Publication Data

Allan, Christian B.
      Life without bread : how a low-carbohydrate diet can save your life /
    Christian B. Allan and Wolfgang Lutz.
          p.   cm.
      Includes bibliographical information and index.
      ISBN 0-658-00170-1 (paper)
      1. Low-carbohydrate diet.   I. Lutz, Wolfgang, 1913–   .   II. Title.

   RM237.73 .A455   2000
   613.2'83—dc21   00-030507

   6 7 8 9 10 11 12 13 14   DOC/DOC   0 9 8 7 6 5 4 3

ISBN 0-658-00170-1

Interior design by Robert S. Tinnon Design

McGraw-Hill books are available at special quantity discounts to use as premiums and sales promotions, or for use in corporate training programs. For more information, please write to the Director of Special Sales, Professional Publishing, McGraw-Hill, Two Penn Plaza, New York, NY 10121-2298. Or contact your local bookstore.

The purpose of this book is to educate. It is sold with the understanding that the publisher and author shall have neither liability nor responsibility for any injury caused or alleged to be caused by the information contained in this book. While every effort has been made to ensure its accuracy, the book's contents should not be construed as medical advice. Each person's health needs are unique. To obtain recommendations appropriate to your particular situation, please consult a qualified health care provider.

This book is printed on acid-free paper.

Contents

Foreword

THE PRINCIPAL NUTRITIONAL ADVICE OF *Life Without Bread* is to limit dietary carbohydrates. In this approach, dietary proteins and fats are correspondingly increased to achieve a balance of calories from fresh, whole foods. This sensible and reasonable advice is based on the observations that Dr. Lutz made during his treatment of thousands of patients with many different diseases throughout his long career as an internist in Austria. It is also based on a large amount of current scientific and medical data published throughout the world. Observations of the benefit of low-carbohydrate nutrition are explored beginning with Herodotus in the fifth century B.C., continuing with Savarin and Banting in the nineteenthth century, and culminating with Steffanson and Price in the twentieth century. Moreover, the approach in *Life Without Bread* is thoroughly compatible with current knowledge of nutrition in the Paleolithic era of human evolution.

The so-called "diseases of Western civilization"—heart disease, obesity, hypertension, diabetes, cancer, dental caries, and others—became pervasive in human populations of developed nations during the twentieth century primarily because of the consumption of a diet containing refined carbohydrates, especially white flour and sugar. The development of the homocysteine theory of arteriosclerosis during the past three decades explains the origin of arteriosclerosis and heart disease as a deficiency of three B vitamins: vitamin B_6, folic acid, and vitamin B_{12}. Epidemiological and clinical studies, such as the Framingham Heart Study, the Nurses' Health Study, the Nutrition Canada Study, the Physicians' Health Study, and many more, have proven that deficiencies of these B vitamins lead to elevation of blood homocysteine levels and increased mortality from coronary heart disease. These same studies also indicate that animal fat is not detrimental to human health. The reason for dietary deficiencies of these B vitamins is destruction of these sensitive vitamins during milling of grains into white flour, extraction of sugar from plants, and other types of harsh food processing. The fact that vitamin B_{12} is only obtained from animal foods suggests that the recent decrease in animal food consumption accompanied by high-carbohydrate diets may be responsible for B_{12} deficiencies. Consumption of refined carbohydrates and other processed foods leads to deficiencies of other B vitamins and micronutrients in developed countries, contributing in a major way to "diseases of Western civilization."

Beginning with observations of elevated cholesterol and lipid levels of victims of vascular disease and the production of fibrolipid plaques in the arteries of animals fed cholesterol, the cholesterol hypothesis was developed in the early twentieth century to explain the origin of vascular disease. As pointed out in *Life Without Bread*, the hypothesis that dietary cholesterol is responsible for elevation of blood cholesterol has never been proven. An unfortunate consequence of the unproven and outmoded cholesterol hypothesis has been the misguided dietary advice given to the public by various governmental agencies and professional societies to consume a low-fat low-cholesterol diet. By restricting dietary fats, meats, and dairy foods, the public has turned to consuming carbohydrates, as advised by the Food Pyramid promulgated by the U. S. Department of Agriculture. The current epidemic of obesity, diabetes and hypertension among adults and children in the United States is a consequence of overconsumption of carbohydrates, especially refined grain foods. According to the nutritional advice of *Life Without Bread*, restriction of dietary carbohydrates will counteract the increased susceptibility to these "diseases of Western civilization." Decreased dietary carbohydrates will decrease excessive insulin secretion and insulin resistance and will increase the amount of vitamin B_6, folic acid, and vitamin B_{12} from fresh, whole foods, preventing numerous problems including elevation of blood homo-cysteine levels and vascular disease susceptibility.

Improvement in dietary quality, as recommended in *Life Without Bread*, offers the best chance to reduce many of the current health problems associated with Western civilization.

KILMER S. McCULLY, M.D.
Providence, Rhode Island
February 2000

Acknowledgments

I OWE A GREAT DEBT TO WOLFGANG LUTZ for providing some of the most comprehensive long-term data on low-carbohydrate nutrition ever accumulated by one individual. It is his evidence from more than forty years of clinical practice that makes *Life Without Bread* so powerful and difficult to ignore.

I would also like to thank Thomas Nufert for his invaluable insights into nutrition and disease. It was at his insistence that I began exploring the medical and biochemical relevance of low-carbohydrate nutrition.

A special thank-you goes to my wife, Jenny, for her help in editing the manuscript and her constant support. She, more than anyone, has made this book possible.

I wish to thank many of the teachers, professors, and researchers I have been associated with over the years. Although some did not agree with the premise of *Life Without Bread*, they compelled me to fully evaluate the alternatives.

I extend my sincerest thank-you to Peter Hoffman, Senior Editor of Keats Publishing. Peter has been a valuable guide in writing this book and a very patient editor. His experience and suggestions have contributed significantly to my ability to finish this book, and his friendship is appreciated.

CHRISTIAN B. ALLAN, PH.D.

My first book was written and published in Germany in 1967. Its title, *Leben Ohne Brot*, translates into the title of this book: *Life Without Bread*. I wish to acknowledge Dr. E. Idris and Verlag for their early interest in my nutritional findings and research, and for the publication of *Leben Ohne Brot*.

I am extremely grateful to Chris Allan for his initial contact with me and for keeping the pledge he made to me in Austria, that he would write an English language *Life Without Bread*. His dedication and hard work are the reason this book came to be.

I wish to thank the people at Keats Publishing who have been associated with this project and the many associates that I have worked with in my long career. Their research and belief in low-carbohydrate nutrition has made a tremendous impact on my life.

WOLFGANG LUTZ, M.D.

Introduction

Over the last few years, there has been a resurgence of interest in low-carbohydrate nutrition as the best way to lose weight and maintain health. As with most ideas that contradict conventional mainstream theories, low-carbohydrate nutrition generates considerable controversy. Unfortunately for all of us, the truth about nutrition is not always dominated by what is actually healthful, but often by special interests, ego, and a lack of proper education needed to evaluate the available information. Equally important, most people who are proponents of a "pet" theory have not taken the time to evaluate contradictory information in an unbiased fashion. They often refuse to consider the alternatives, even though there may be good evidence for these different ideas.

The low-fat theory of nutrition is at center stage as I write this introduction, even though it has not stopped the incidence of degenerative disease from skyrocketing over the last thirty or more years. The information presented in this book will clearly show that the low-fat theory of health and disease is wrong.

Life Without Bread convincingly outlines the unmistakable benefits of low-carbohydrate nutrition. It presents actual data from the medical files of Dr. Wolfgang Lutz, who has used low-carbohydrate nutrition on many thousands of patients in Austria and Germany for more than forty years. He has put together powerful evidence that proper human nutrition should emphasize high animal fat and protein, not high carbohydrates. A mountain of information is presented here—far beyond anything ever before published in the United States on this topic. This book shows how low-carbohydrate nutrition can actually reverse—and in some cases cure—many different diseases.

However, Dr. Lutz didn't always champion a low-carbohydrate diet. In fact, both of us were, at some stage of our careers, proponents of the low-fat diet. But as our own health began to fade early in our lives, we had to explore other nutritional alternatives. The results of our journey to vibrant health follow in the pages of this book.

We have written *Life Without Bread* to help people achieve optimal health. It is our hope that even those who are adamantly against low-carbohydrate nutrition will take the time to read this book because much of the information will be new to American readers. Our intention is to dig deeply into the lifestyle changes necessary for all of us to live happy, healthy lives. We also hope that the many authors who publish books on this subject will use our information to help support the wisdom of low-carbohydrate nutrition.

So sit back, grab a handful of beef jerky and a glass of whole milk, and enjoy. We believe this journey will be one of the most important ones of your life, as it has been for us, our relatives and friends, and the thousands of people who have already benefited from the power of low-carbohydrate nutrition.

CHRISTIAN B. ALLAN, PH.D.
Brookeville, Maryland
January 2000

CHAPTER ONE

What Is Low-Carbohydrate Nutrition?

CONTRARY TO CURRENT POPULAR WISDOM, it is carbohydrates, not fat, that contribute to many dietary related diseases.

You may be wondering what carbohydrates are, how many carbohydrates are in different foods, and how one can realistically maintain low-carbohydrate nutrition for the rest of one's life? Let's begin with a closer look at the components of foods. There are three types of macronutrients that constitute most of what we consume: proteins, fats, and carbohydrates.

PROTEINS

Proteins are the most abundant component of our cells and tissue. The name *protein* comes from the Greek word *proteios*, meaning "of first importance." They perform an amazing array of functions throughout our body. They include enzymes, antibodies, hormones, and transport molecules, and are even components of the skeleton. There are twenty common amino acids that constitute most proteins, but there are many less common amino acids that are also important.

However, there are eight amino acids that are essential. Essential means that they must be obtained in the diet because the body cannot make them from other nutrients and raw materials supplied in the diet. In many instances, nutrients can be made from simple building blocks directly within our cells, but the essential nutrients cannot be made in this way. They must be obtained in the diet.

The essential amino acids are valine, lysine, threonine, leucine, isoleucine, tryptophan, phenylalanine, and methionine. These eight amino acids must be consumed in the diet, and animal foods are the only foods that supply all eight in one single source. People who do not eat animal foods run the risk of deficiencies in the essential amino acids. All of them can be obtained from nonanimal foods, but no single plant food contains all eight. Studies have shown that the body needs all of the essential amino acids in the same meal in order to make important proteins. If only a few essential amino acids are supplied, the body does not store them until all of them become available; instead, the amino acids are broken down and eliminated. This is one of many reasons that animal foods are very important in the human diet.

FATS

Fats (sometimes called *fatty acids* or *lipids*) have many important and diverse functions in the body. They are the primary storage form of energy in the body and supply the most energy to our cells. The heart, for example, uses primarily fat for its energy. Fats are the major constituents of cell membranes. Cell membrane integrity and permeability to various biomolecules is critical for proper metabolic functions. Finally, members of a select class of lipids function as hormones.

There are two known essential fatty acids: linoleic acid and alpha-linolenic acid. These fatty acids are classified as unsaturated. Contrary to popular wisdom, saturated fat is actually very healthy. We will explore this in detail throughout the book, but a little should be said about it here.

The terms *saturated* and *unsaturated* are used to denote the amount of hydrogen atoms that are contained on each carbon atom in the fat molecule. The more unsaturated the fat, the fewer hydrogen atoms there are. A consequence of fewer hydrogen atoms is that unsaturated fats are chemically more reactive, while saturated fats are chemically more stable. Why does this matter? Saturated fatty acids are more resistant to oxidation, which means membranes that contain more saturated fat are less susceptible to oxidation. Many studies have shown that the types of fat associated with membranes are related to the types of fat consumed.

Research has repeatedly emphasized the value of antioxidants, yet seems to have overlooked the fact that, unlike unsaturated fat, saturated fat alone can resist oxidation. Saturated fat does not require a secondary molecule, such as an antioxidant, to eliminate the negative effect of oxidation.

The two essential fatty acids can be found in varying degrees in all animal foods, as well as in nuts and vegetable oils. Animal foods tend to supply equal amounts of the two essential fatty acids, whereas vegetable oils typically contain predominantly one or the other of the essential fatty acids.

CARBOHYDRATES

Carbohydrates are primarily used as an energy source. They are also often attached to proteins to enhance the recognition and specific transport properties of proteins. Some forms of carbohydrates are part of cartilage, and there are a few known carbohydrates that help eliminate toxins from the body.

To our knowledge, there has never been an essential carbohydrate discovered. Every carbohydrate your body needs can be made from either protein or fat. This is not a point we dwell on because there is ample evidence to support the fact that low-carbohydrate nutrition is very healthy and is the proper nutrition for humans, regardless of whether carbohydrates are essential or not. It is interesting, however, that even in nature there is not much specific dietary necessity placed on carbohydrates for humans.

Carbohydrates are classified as either simple or complex. Examples of simple carbohydrates are sugar and honey. Complex carbohydrates are found in many foods, including potatoes, bread, and cereals. You probably have heard the term "starch" associated with potatoes. This is just another way of saying that potatoes contain carbohydrates.

As far as food is concerned, carbohydrates are simply different forms of sugar. Simple carbohydrates contain one sugar molecule, or two sugar molecules linked together. Complex carbohydrates contain many sugar molecules linked together, called polysaccharides. All of these act like sugar in our bodies. Our stomach and intestinal juices can break apart the complex carbohydrates, and our bodies see them as a simple sugar. Complex carbohydrates may be absorbed into our bloodstream more slowly than simple carbohydrates, but they still break down into simple sugars. It is the cumulative effect of eating large amounts of carbohydrates that can lead to a host of health problems.

To repeat this important point, when you eat any carbohydrate you are essentially eating sugar. The implications of this will be discussed later, but for now don't be fooled by those who say that some carbohydrates are healthy because they are *complex* carbohydrates.

A Utilizable Carbohydrate

By "utilizable," we mean the amount of carbohydrate that actually gets into the bloodstream when we eat certain foods. Let's look at a few examples. A medium apple that weighs approximately 100 grams contains about 12 grams of utilizable carbohydrate; in other words, it is 12 percent utilizable carbohydrate. That means that when you eat this apple, you actually eat about 12 grams of carbohydrate. However, if you eat 100 grams of white bread (four or five slices), you actually consume about 50 grams of carbohydrates because white bread has more than 50 percent utilizable carbohydrate. Light beer, on the other hand, contains around 5 percent utilizable carbohydrate (in addition to alcohol), so if you drink 250 grams of beer (about half of a glass, or 8 ounces), you would be getting about 12 grams of carbohydrate.

The take-home message for healthful low-carbohydrate eating is the following:

Restrict all carbohydrates to 72 utilizable grams per day.
Eat as much of any other foods as you wish.

That's all there is to it. There is no need to memorize complicated formulas. The following pages describe our low-carbohydrate nutritional program in more detail.

THE BASICS

Permitted Foods

- Fish
- Any type of animal meat (beef, pork, chicken, lamb), sausage, cold cuts
- Eggs
- Cheese, sour cream, cream cheese, plain yogurt (without sugar), cream, milk (in moderate amounts)
- All kinds of animal fats
- Salads, leaves and stems of vegetables (asparagus, brussels sprouts, cauliflower, lettuce, cabbage, broccoli), cucumbers, avocados, tomatoes (in moderate amounts)
- Alcoholic beverages (only unsweetened, and in sensible amounts)
- Nuts (in moderate amounts)

These foods can be prepared any way you like: fried, baked, roasted, broiled, barbecued, or steamed. Small amounts of breading and sauces don't count toward the 72 grams of carbohydrate per day. Larger amounts will have to be counted, particularly if the sauce is mostly sugar-based (beware of typical barbecue sauces and sweet-and-sour sauces).

Restricted Foods

- All carbohydrate-containing foods (breads, pastas, cereals, grains, potatoes, pastries, bagels)
- Sweet fruits
- Sweetened foods of all kinds (yogurt, drinks, desserts, candy)
- Dried fruits

Now, this sounds easy, doesn't it? You can eat as much fat and protein as you want, as long as you keep the carbohydrates to 72 grams or less per day. And don't skimp on fat. It is important to eat plenty of fat when you reduce carbohydrates; don't rely on protein only.

You're probably thinking: "If I reduce carbohydrate to 72 grams per day, and I eat unlimited amounts of fat and protein, won't I gain weight?" Perhaps. However, one of the wonderful consequences of reducing your carbohydrate consumption to a very low amount is that you won't have the appetite to eat too much fat and protein. You will get full very quickly and will be able to naturally stop eating. The effect is completely opposite when it comes to sugar and carbohydrates: "I'll just have one more potato chip, pretzel, or piece of candy"; "Just one more of those cookies and I'll stop"; or "I might as well finish the whole bag so they won't go stale!" Most people are actually addicted to carbohydrates; to overcome this addiction one must eat plenty of fatty foods to kill the urge for more and more carbohydrates.

Any foods that contain virtually no carbohydrate can be eaten freely: meats, cheese, fish, eggs, and butter. Foods such as these contain almost no carbohydrate, so they won't count toward your 72 grams per day.

To make this program easy to follow, we have chosen a special term to describe the amount of utilizable carbohydrate in any given weight of food. That term is bread unit (or BU). The term *bread unit* was introduced in Vienna in the beginning of the nineteenth century for diabetics. At that time, it was already known that diabetics needed to restrict their intake of carbohydrates. A half of a roll that weighed 20 grams contained 12 grams of utilizable carbohydrate, and this was considered 1 bread unit (BU). We have adopted this terminology in this book, hence the title, *Life Without Bread*. Exhibit 1.1 lists the BUs present in a number of common foods.

Exhibit 1.1 Bread Units (BUs) and Their Equivalents

Bread Units (BUs)	Selected Food
1 bread unit	1 tablespoon sugar, honey, or flour
"	4 teaspoons dry white or brown rice
"	¼ cup dry pasta (all kinds)
"	1 slice of bread (wheat, rye, or white)
"	¼ of a bagel
"	½ of a tortilla
"	2 tablespoons dried beans
"	⅔ cup peas
"	½ of a medium potato
"	⅓ of a medium yam
"	1 cup broccoli
"	½ grapefruit
"	1 medium apple
"	handful of grapes
"	⅔ cup strawberries
"	1 ounce dried fruits (2 tablespoons)
"	1 cup whole or low-fat milk
"	½ cup fruit juices (4 ounces)
"	½ cup soda (4 ounces)
"	1 cup beer (8 ounces)

Each bread unit is 12 grams of utilizable carbohydrate. Under this program, you are allowed 6 BUs per day:

12 grams × 6 BUs = 72 total grams of utilizable carbohydrate

You can eat these any way you like. If you want to have pastry, milk, candy, or pasta, you can. But you can only eat 6 BUs total (or less) per day. In the back of the book we have made a table that shows the amount of BUs contained in many common foods. The numbers were calculated from the total carbohydrate content of the foods and then adjusted for utilizable carbohydrate. Remember, foods that have little or no carbohydrate are not included in the table because these can be eaten in any amounts. If there are foods that are not shown in the table, you can use any published carbohydrate table and simply remember that 12 grams of utilizable carbohydrate equals 1 BU.

In the beginning you will have to consult the table often to see how many BUs you are eating, but after a while you will simply know from experience.

CHAPTER TWO

An Old Idea: The History of Low-Carbohydrate Nutrition

IF YOU ASK TEN PEOPLE HOW NUTRITION contributes to disease and poor health, you would probably get ten different answers. We can hardly blame anyone for being confused. There are so many different approaches to nutrition that it becomes difficult to trust any of them.

For instance, vegetarians believe that only food of plant origin is healthy and object to all foods derived from animals. Some vegetarians eat only fruit and vegetables; others eat all plant-derived food products, even if they contain lots of starch, such as bread, potatoes, and rice. Some consider milk and milk products harmless but believe that meat and fat are detrimental to their health. There also are vegetarians who only eat raw vegetables because they believe that only uncooked plants are wholesome. The list goes on.

Other people believe that the increasing use of artificial fertilizer, pesticides, and insecticides has led to the increase of many of today's modern diseases. This is a reasonable idea, but has it been proven or is it just an opinion? Some people think that food from animals raised without the use of antibiotics and hormones is the only way to guarantee the continued health of mankind. Ironically, we often see these same people eating a lot of sweets.

So many people base their nutritional ideas on hearsay, on a specific study covered by the popular media, or on what they are told by their physician. Here's a typical scenario: You read a newspaper story or magazine article that says fat is unhealthy. You relate this information to some friends, and they tell others. Pretty soon it is "the truth" and everyone believes it. For many years, it has been "understood" that fat is bad for people. The newspapers and magazines say it. The television shows say it. Your friends say it. The medical establishment says it.

But don't you think that this approach is rather limited? What real evidence have you evaluated?

The reality is that most people don't have the time and appropriate background to properly investigate the scientific and medical literature that is available. Instead, the typical consumer relies on "experts" to explain what is healthy or unhealthy. Unfortunately, many of these experts are themselves living in an illusory world. They tend to focus only on what they have been brought up on or trained to believe, without removing the bias that exists in their perceptions.

We followed the same approach for many years. But then we decided to examine critically what is really happening with our health. Both of us began to question the validity of theories that had so far not lived up to their promise. Our own health began to deteriorate even though we strictly adhered to a low-fat diet.

In our opinion, carbohydrates are to a large extent responsible for most human illnesses. We have sought to obtain evidence for this idea, not only from observations on ourselves and our own families and friends, but from the many thousands of patients in one author's medical practice, as well as from a plethora of research that supports this conclusion.

PIONEERS OF THE LOW-CARBOHYDRATE DIET

Herodotus

Observations recorded throughout modern history reflect the benefit of low-carbohydrate nutrition. Herodotus[1] tells of the meeting between a Persian delegation and the king of Ethiopia in the fifth century B.C., and of the curiosity of the Ethiopian king concerning Cambyses, the Persian king:

> Finally [the Ethiopian king] came to the wine and, having learnt the process of its manufacture, drank some and found it delicious; then, for a last question, he asked what the Persian king ate and what was the greatest age that Persians could attain. Getting in reply an account of the nature and cultivation of wheat, and hearing that the Persian king ate bread, and that people in Persia did not commonly live beyond eighty, he said he was not surprised that anyone who ate dung should die so soon, adding that the Persians would doubtlessly die younger still, if they did not keep themselves going with that drink—and here he pointed to the wine—the one thing in which he admitted the superiority of the Persians.

The Persians, in their turn, asked the Ethiopian king how long the Ethiopians lived and what they ate, and were told that most of them lived to be 120, and some even more, and that they ate boiled meat and drank milk.

For the increasing population of the Earth at the beginning of the agricultural age, the consumption of cereals, and thus a life *with* bread, became unavoidable. Every achievement of mankind, whether connected with craftsmanship, art, industry, science, religion, or politics, depends upon a certain degree of urbanization and of population density. Without these, a rational distribution of labor and specialization into professions would not be possible.

Before the introduction of modern methods of animal breeding, there was no means of feeding large numbers of people in a small area other than with cereals and other carbohydrates, all products of agriculture. Thus cereals, fruits, and vegetables came to form the basis of human nutrition. In the absence of scientific knowledge, the diseases of civilization were regarded as a necessary God-sent evil and not due to an improper diet or to other harmful effects of civilization itself. Only gradually have the real causes come to light.

Anthelme Brillat Savarin

Renowned the world over today for having been a king among gourmets, Anthelme Brillat Savarin (1755–1826) achieved distinction as a judge in the Supreme French Court in Paris. In his book *Physiologie du gout*,[2] which appeared in 1825, an entire chapter is devoted to excess weight. In addition to being a lawyer, he was greatly interested in medicine, physiology, and chemistry, and already was well aware of the connections between carbohydrates and obesity. The following quotation, translated from the German edition of Savarin's book, indicates his opinion as to the causes of being overweight:

> This is, in fact, an infallible method both for preventing excessive corpulence, and for reducing it if this state should already have been reached. . . . [It] consists in a diet based upon the most reliable principles of physics and chemistry and suited of the desired end. Such a diet must take into consideration the most common and decisive causes of obesity. Since it can be taken as proven that fat formation in man and animals is due to flour and starch, the logical conclusion to be drawn is that more or less complete abstinence from flour- and starch-containing foods will lead to a reduction in girth.

William Banting

In the year 1862, an English ear specialist, Dr. Harvey, was consulted by a very corpulent coffin-maker, William Banting, who was becoming deaf. Harvey suggested, with striking success, that Banting refrain from eating carbohydrates. Banting's weight then dropped by about 50 pounds in one year. He had previously only been able to go down the stairs backward and was so delighted with his new figure that, in 1864, he published a small booklet at his own expense,[3] recommending the diet to all sufferers from excess weight. He wrote (according to R. Mackarness):[4]

For the sake of argument and illustration I will presume that certain articles of ordinary diet, however beneficial in youth, are prejudicial in advanced life, like beans to a horse, whose common ordinary food is hay and corn. It may be useful food occasionally, under peculiar circumstances, but detrimental as a constancy. I will, therefore, adopt the analogy, and call such food human beans. The items from which I was advised to abstain as much as possible were bread, sugar, beer, and potatoes, which had been the main and, I thought, innocent elements of my existence, or at all events they had for many years been adopted freely These, said my excellent adviser, contain starch and saccharine matter, tending to create fat, and should be avoided altogether. . . . I can now confidently say that QUANTITY of diet may be safely left to the natural appetite; and that it is the QUALITY only, which is essential to abate and cure corpulence.

Banting published his *Letters on Corpulence* privately in 1864 because he feared (not without reason as it turned out) that the editor of the medical journal *The Lancet*, to whom he first thought of submitting the piece, would refuse to publish anything "from an insignificant individual without some special introduction."

Weston A. Price

During the 1920s and 1930s, Weston Price and his wife, Florence, traveled around the world to study primitive populations. Price, a dentist, was convinced that changing from primitive foods—foods to which humans had adapted over thousands of years—to modern processed foods was a key to degenerative diseases of modern civilization. He made remarkable discoveries in his years of travel. He began his research by looking at the teeth, mouth, and jaws of primitive people. He compared them to the same races that had become "modernized."

What he encountered was remarkable in its simplicity: Time and again he found that only one generation was necessary to see major changes in jaw malformation, dental cavities, and crooked teeth. Without exception, the people who ate meat, milk, unprocessed grains, and vegetables, were the healthier individuals. In 1939, he published his remarkable observations in a book entitled *Nutrition and Physical Degeneration*. Today, the sixth edition is available,[5] and it is an important book for anyone who wants to learn more about nutrition and disease.

Price never specifically recommended reducing carbohydrates. He did state many times that sugars, pastries, breads, and processed foods of all kinds were the dietary components responsible for the deterioration of mankind's health. He also expressed his concerns that unless humans return to the ancestral diet rich in fat and animal foods, mankind will continue to deteriorate as a species. He determined that "fat-soluble activators" were not available in modern carbohydrate-based diets. These fat-soluble activators are available only in animal foods.

The legacy of Weston Price and his invaluable observations still remains today. A foundation has been set-up to keep people up-to-date about the myths surrounding the low-fat theory of health.[6]

Vilhjalmur Stefansson

Vilhjalmur Stefansson, an Icelander by birth, was a physician and anthropologist. He spent fifteen years traveling on foot and horseback, by dogsled and canoe from settlement to settlement among the Canadian Eskimos. He slept, lived, dressed, and ate like the natives. As a doctor, it did not escape his notice that, apart from a few berries preserved in whale oil, and a little moss from the stomachs of the animals that were hunted for food, these Eskimos existed entirely upon animal matter, yet suffered none of the dreaded diseases of "civilized" peoples. They were not plagued by elevated blood pressure, coronary infarction, strokes, cancer, nor—which particularly struck Stefansson—by excess weight, although they ate large quantities of food and consumed an amount of calories that would have surely resulted in obesity if the same amount of calories came from carbohydrates. Eskimo women had none of the typical gynecological complaints: no difficult births, no complications in pregnancy, or problems in breast-feeding. Above all, the Eskimos lived in a state of mental balance, free from the aggravations and dissension that form part of today's typical existence. Of course, the isolation and seclusion in which the Eskimos lived could have been partly responsible for this.

When he finally returned to the United States, Stefansson published a number of books on his experiences in the Canadian north, including *The Friendly Arctic, Not By Bread Alone,* and *The Fat of the Land.*[7]

In his last book, *Cancer, Disease of Civilization,*[8] which appeared shortly before his death, he revealed documentary evidence that showed that, prior to their contact with American civilization, the Eskimos (like other primitive peoples) did not suffer from cancer. At the missions erected near the native whaling stations, the missionaries kept exact records of the causes of death among the Eskimos. Stefansson was able to contact many of these ministers, or their widows, and from the material he collected it did indeed appear that the traditional meat-eating Eskimo did not suffer from cancer.

As civilization reached the natives of Canada at the turn of the century, they, too, began to consume carbohydrates, and it was then that the diseases connected with our civilization also began to appear. Today, Eskimos suffer from obesity, dental caries, complications in childbirth and nursing, gynecological problems, elevated blood pressure, atherosclerosis, coronary infarction, cerebral strokes, and cancer.

It is the same observation made by Weston Price: Civilizations that begin to consume Western foods begin to get significant increases in the Western diseases. The fallacy surrounding these observations is that Western "modern" diets are high in fat, when in fact they contain an excess of carbohydrate and are lower in fat and protein compared to diets of primitive populations. It is obvious, however, that these diseases turn up with a certain degree of latency, for example, diabetes only after the elapse of several generations.

Because Stefansson was an anthropologist as well as an adventurer and physician, this rare combination enabled him to grasp connections that had been long overlooked. He was the first to recognize that it was not the racial origins of the Eskimo that accounted for the absence of Western disease but rather their primitive form of nutrition. He saw that, in human developmental phases, and up to the end of the Ice Age, all mankind, like the Eskimo, lived almost solely on animal foods.

The reaction in scientific circles to Stefansson's books was both deprecatory and incredulous. The minds of the era were immersed in metabolic investigations and the merits of vitamins; it seemed impossible that anyone could live for years without fresh fruit and vegetables. Stefansson was quite bluntly accused of publishing fiction and uncritical reports. This is often the response even today, when theories that fail to deliver are propped up by ego and alternate possibilities are ignored.

So Stefansson and his earlier traveling companion, Karsten Anderson, resolved to subject themselves to an experiment, which was to be carried out under supervision at the Bellevue Hospital in New York, and directed by the well-known metabolic expert, Eugene Dubois. During the many years he had accompanied Stefansson in the far north, Anderson always felt extremely well, but in the ensuing years, as a farmer in Florida and on a typical high-carbohydrate American diet, he was continually ailing.

Both men were admitted to the hospital in 1928 and embarked upon a diet consisting exclusively of fresh meat. Vegetables, fruit, eggs, milk, and milk products were excluded. The beginning of the experiment was observed by a group of European physiologists, who happened to be in New York at the time. They postponed their return to Europe by several weeks in order, as they thought, to observe the onset of scurvy and other symptoms of deficiency in the experimental subjects.

They were on a meat diet for months, but no signs of illness were detected. Stefansson occasionally left the enclave on various journeys but adhered strictly to the diet, whereas Anderson spent the whole year in the metabolic unit of Bellevue Hospital. He, at least, ought to have sickened, but instead he felt extraordinarily well and lost his excess weight and the other complaints that had worried him in Florida.

At the end of the experimental year, Dubois commented that "the most remarkable thing about the experiment was that nothing remarkable occurred."

The scientific world took note of the experiment, but the only real consequence was an attempt to employ a low-carbohydrate diet for weight-reducing purposes,[9–12] which still left open the connection of other diseases to excess carbohydrate consumption.

About this time, scientific articles began to appear reporting the value of fat in losing weight. Although this was a breakthrough as far as the concept of the purely caloric contribution of various food constituents to body weight is concerned, only Stefansson himself appeared to be aware of the significance of a low-carbohydrate diet, even if he did not state it outright. In fact, his wife later wrote to Dr. Lutz, when President Eisenhower suffered his coronary infarction, Stefansson returned to his "friendly Arctic diet" and adhered to it until his death. Apparently, Stefansson, too, was convinced of the value of this type of diet, not only in treating obesity but also in combating other diseases of civilization.

LOW-CARBOHYDRATE NUTRITION TODAY

Although Stefansson has shown that the low-carbohydrate-eating Eskimos didn't suffer from all of our modern diseases, even though they reached a significantly high age, subsequent physicians who believed in the benefit of low-carbohydrate eating concentrated mostly on obesity, one of the diseases most unyielding to dietary therapy. Not a single book on low-carbohydrate diets has put the emphasis where it belongs: on the underlying cause of most disease. There is a powerful connection between malfunctioning hormones and the beginning stages of disease development, and low-carbohydrate nutrition can alleviate and often reverse this metabolic imbalance. We will discuss this fully in chapter 3.

Many books have been written about the benefits of low-carbohydrate nutrition in human health. The first book, however, to present clear evidence that diseases can be successfully treated by carbohydrate restriction was published in 1967 by one author of this book, Wolfgang Lutz, M.D.[13] His book, now in its fourteenth edition, was based on evidence obtained in his medical practice using low-carbohydrate nutrition to treat diseases. Unfortunately for America, this book was only published in German, and little attention was paid to it in the English-speaking countries. Subsequent books about low-carbohydrate nutrition did not draw on the powerful medical evidence included in this groundbreaking book.

In his 1972 book, *Sweet and Dangerous*,[14] John Yudkin, M.D., looked at the relationship between sugar intake and disease. Dr. Herman Tarnower mentioned many symptoms that are amenable to treatment with reduced carbohydrates in his best-selling book, *The Complete Scarsdale Medical Diet*.[15] Barry Sears, Ph.D., reported in his popular book, *The Zone*,[16] about the enhanced success of athletes who adopted a reduced carbohydrate diet; he also cited the role a low-carbohydrate diet played in the successful treatment of multiple sclerosis. The two physicians Michael and Mary Eades have also reported on their therapeutic successes with low-carbohydrate nutrition.[17] The four authors of *Sugar Busters* discuss the influence of insulin and glucagon on health and the relationship of these hormones to carbohydrate consumption.[18] Dr. Robert Atkins, the most successful author on low-carbohydrate nutrition in the United States, and perhaps the world, concentrates mostly on obesity, but he also has observed that low-carbohydrate nutrition and a diet rich in animal foods actually reduces cholesterol in the blood.[19] Ann Louise Gittleman, M.S., has written numerous books about the myths surrounding low-fat diets and weight. Her most recent book,

Eat Fat, Lose Weight,[20] discusses the importance of the essential fatty acids in health and weight control. In his recent book, *Your Fat Can Make You Thin,*[21] Calvin Ezrin, M.D., presents an informed and important evaluation of weight loss from the perspective of a trained and experienced endocrinologist. His book topples one of the myths surrounding low-carbohydrate diets, namely that ketosis is an unhealthy state. People from all over the world are aware of the benefits of low-carbohydrate nutrition. In his book *Optimal Nutrition,*[22] Jan Kwasniewski, M.D., a doctor in Poland, shows that high-fat low-carbohydrate, diets promote healing of many diseases. He has used this nutrition for therapy to treat diseases, just as we will present in this book. Barry Groves, a British researcher and engineer, presents a powerful argument to consume a high animal-fat, low-carbohydrate diet. In his book, *Eat Fat, Get Thin,*[23] he derails many of the ideas surrounding disease and fat consumption.

These authors and others all deserve some praise because of the strength of character required to report on a nutritional theory that goes against the powerful establishment that supports the low-fat theory. It is true that most of these books offer little more than anecdotal evidence, but the message that low-carbohydrate nutrition supports overall improved health is loud and clear. However, many of these authors do not go far enough. They still support the idea that saturated fat is unhealthy in large amounts, when in fact just the opposite is true.

It is our sincere hope that this book will substantially augment all of their arguments, because we now offer the most powerful evidence in support of low-carbohydrate nutrition ever published in the United States It is time for all the people who have supported low-carbohydrate nutrition to combine resources and information and educate the public to eat a low-carbohydrate, high-fat diet. Saturated animal fat and protein are the cure that stares us in the face. Let's not lose sight of this simple solution to many of our modern diseases.

CHAPTER THREE

Carbohydrates and Hormones: Balance Your Way to Optimal Health

SIMPLY PUT, CARBOHYDRATE CONSUMPTION has a direct effect on hormonal balance and, therefore, a direct effect on overall health. Yet most endocrinologists, those physicians who specialize in hormones, do not recognize the fact that carbohydrate consumption is that major dietary source of hormonal imbalance. Instead, multiple hormone supplements and various other drugs are prescribed to alleviate conditions that often can be resolved merely by a reduction of carbohydrates in the diet.

There are numerous concepts that must be understood in order to appreciate the profound effects that eating too many carbohydrates has on our health. We will examine some of these by looking at different diseases that are known to be directly related to hormonal imbalances. We will explain hormones, anabolic and catabolic processes, and the endocrine balance. In future chapters, these ideas will be related to different glandular disorders and degenerative diseases: diabetes, obesity, problematic sexual maturation, hyperthyroidism, heart disease, and cancer.

HORMONES

Hormones are molecules that perform the major regulatory functions in the body. They are secreted by various glands, and thus glandular disorders are really disorders related to hormones.

Hormones have many functions as the body's messengers. In scientific language, they are referred to as signalers. They are so important that all other signals within the cells are ignored when a hormonal signal is sent. Not only do hormones send signals throughout the body to keep the communication lines open, but they also can help perform specific biochemical functions. For example, if you cut yourself, your body sends out signals to repair and replace tissue. Growth hormone is associated with new tissue repair.

During puberty, hormones play a role in the growth and maturation of the sex organs, a process ultimately related to reproduction and the cycle of life. These hormones are called the sex hormones. There are hormones that regulate the immune system, hormones that signal the body to store sugar in the liver for later use as energy, and hormones that cause stored fat to be burned as fuel when needed.

INSULIN

What is responsible for so many of the disturbances seen in high-carbohydrate eaters? The answer begins with the hormone insulin. Insulin is perhaps the single most important hormone in our body because it is the one that responds directly to carbohydrates in our diet. Remember this very important point:

*Our body's primary response to carbohydrates is
the release of insulin into the bloodstream.*

This fundamental detail is often ignored when people insist that what matters is not what type of calorie you eat, but how much you eat. We cannot continue to ignore the fact that our body responds to foods differently, and carbohydrates bring about a disproportionately larger increase of insulin, compared to fat and protein.

In 1922, Banting and Best discovered that insulin is produced in the pancreas, in cells called beta cells. When you eat carbohydrates—simple or complex—insulin is released into the blood-stream to perform two main functions:

1. Insulin's primary responsibility is to transport glucose into the cells to be used for energy. Glucose is a simple sugar formed from the breakdown of all carbohydrates in the intestines and stomach.
2. The second function of insulin is to help convert and store the sugar as glycogen in the liver and as fat in fat cells. The fat is stored in the form of triglycerides (also called triacyl-glycerides) in adipose tissue.

Another hormone, called *glucagon,* has the opposite effect of insulin. It is the body's messenger to metabolize, or use, fat. When insulin levels are low for a long enough period of time, glucagon should be released to begin burning fat in the form of stored triglycerides. There is a balance between insulin and glucagon, and they work in opposite ways to maintain neutrality in the body's storage and usage of fat. If your body begins to store fat, this means that the hormone glucagon is not being released into the blood. It can also mean that you are not using all the energy you are supplying. What causes the release of glucagon? This, and many other hormonal functions, are controlled by many factors, but carbohydrate consumption is the primary dietary factor that influences your hormonal balance and, therefore, your overall health.

A METABOLIC BALANCING ACT

The process of making new tissue and new cells and breaking them down is called *metabolism.* You're no doubt familiar with this word, but what does it really mean?

Everything that takes place to maintain life in your organs, tissue, cells, and cellular organelles is lumped into the term "metabolism." This process includes simple things, such as growing fingernails and hair, and complicated things, such as the breakdown of fat for energy. It is a general term used to describe all the biochemical reactions that keep the body alive. Metabolism constitutes the balance between making new tissue and breaking it down.

It wasn't until the 1960s that a theory was proposed to explain exactly how the body balances making and breaking of tissue. This is called the two-component theory, and it originated from studies on animals in veterinary medicine. Dr. Juergen Schole, professor of physiological chemistry at the Veterinary Medical School in Hanover, Germany, and his colleagues Peter Sallmann and G. Harish, performed extensive studies on the effects of carbohydrates on warm-blooded animals.[1] In this theory, each sector of animal tissue, including organs and individual cells, strives to balance the forces that metabolize matter to make energy, as well as the forces that use energy and substrate to build matter. These two forces are now called anabolic (anabolism) and catabolic (catabolism) forces. They comprise two components of overall metabolism.

Anabolic processes are those that build molecules, tissue, and even organs in the body. These reactions represent one side of a very important balancing act that the body is always trying to achieve. The replacement of tissue from an injury is an example of this metabolic process.

Catabolic processes, on the other hand, are those that break down substances into simpler ones. An example would be the breakdown of fat or sugar for use as energy.

Anabolism and catabolism are finely tuned processes that the body always strives to keep in balance. If anabolic processes prevail, the result will be too much building and not enough breaking down. Gaining weight represents excess anabolism. If catabolic reactions dominate the physiology, there will be too much tissue breakdown and a lack of tissue growth when needed.

Hormones are the messengers that strive to keep the body's anabolic and catabolic processes in balance. There are many anabolic and catabolic hormones. Insulin is an anabolic hormone because it

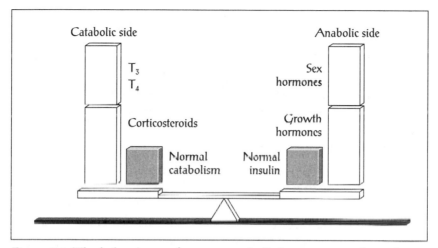

Figure 3.1 The balancing act between anabolic hormones on the right and catabolic hormones on the left. When we eat 6 or fewer BUs (bread units) of carbohydrates per day, we keep hormones in balance.

tends to promote the storage of energy and the buildup of fat. Glucose, which is a small molecule, gets converted to larger molecules by the action of insulin. Thus, insulin promotes the anabolic process of building up. Glucagon is a catabolic hormone. It signals the body to break down larger molecules into smaller ones for use in energy production. Together, these two hormones represent one of your body's many balancing acts.

Figure 3.1 gives you an idea of the hormonal balance that takes place within the body. This "teeter-totter" representation of hormonal balance is simple enough to understand: You can see that if any one of the hormones increases or decreases, relative to the others, an imbalance would occur. The weight would shift to one side, just like a heavier person on one side on a seesaw. Small changes in this balance probably occur every day in all of us, but it is the long-term effect of too much hormone weight on one side of the hormonal teeter-totter that presents the real danger.

The catabolic hormones shown on the left are the glucocorticoids and the T_3 and T_4 hormones. Glucocorticoids are produced in the adrenal cortex and are called steroids. These comprise a class of many hormones, including cortisol and corticosterone.

You probably have heard stories in the media about athletes taking steroids to enhance athletic performance and build muscle. These types of steroids are called anabolic steroids because they promote building of tissue. Steroids are produced naturally from cholesterol, one of the many important functions of cholesterol in our body. We will explore cholesterol and its controversial relationship to heart disease in chapter 6. Steroids' many functions include their effects on protein synthesis and inflammation. They are often prescribed orally to reduce inflammation, and sometimes are injected into injured tissue to alleviate inflammation from acute injuries. The steroid hormones also help regulate the immune system.

The catabolic hormones thyroxine (T_3) and triiodothyronine (T_4) are thyroid hormones that function as general stimulators of many cellular reactions. They contain iodine in their molecules. During puberty and pregnancy, these hormones become elevated, an increase related to the two-component theory. The sex hormones are anabolic hormones, and they naturally increase during puberty and pregnancy. The increase in anabolic sex hormones results in an increase in catabolic hormones. This is done to balance catabolic and anabolic forces. The increase in thyroid function, if accompanied with iodine deficiency, can result in goiter.

On the right side of the teeter-totter are the anabolic hormones: growth hormone; sex hormones, as we just mentioned; and insulin. We have discussed insulin, so let's focus now on the other two types. Growth hormone is a very important hormone that is produced in the pituitary gland. It works to stimulate the growth of cells and tissue, is critically important for tissue integrity at all ages, and represents a major factor for growth throughout childhood. For example, hair growth is maintained by the production of growth hormone. There are many other known "growth factors," some of which we will discuss in chapter 10. Tissue repair from injury and normal aging requires growth hormone.

The sex hormones are another set of anabolic hormones, and they are produced in the gonads of both males and females. Many of the sex hormones also are steroids. Estrogens and progestins are produced in the ovaries. Androgens are produced in the testes. These all work mainly in the maturation and function of sex organs, but they have other important functions as well.

There are many hormones in our body. We chose to focus on those in Figure 3.1 because some of the hormones depicted are related specifically to the diseases we will discuss later in the chapter.

How does all of this relate to carbohydrates and disease? The answer is that too much carbohydrate in the diet disrupts the balancing act between anabolic and catabolic forces because it sends too much insulin to the blood. Since the body will always move to balance anabolic and catabolic reactions, increases in insulin must be dealt with in some way. Figure 3.2 shows what happens to the hormonal teeter-totter if too many carbohydrates are consumed.

Let's take a look at how the body attempts to regain balance between anabolic and catabolic processes and hormones.

In order to return to hormonal balance, either other anabolic hormones must be reduced to make less weight on the anabolic side of the teeter-totter or catabolic hormones must increase to add weight to the catabolic side. Either of these events contains a potential problem and can lead to different diseases.

On the anabolic side, the levels of growth hormone will often decrease to achieve hormonal balance. This is a well-known condition with people who have Type 2 diabetes, which we will discuss in chapter 4. Diminished amounts of growth hormone affect the immune system and the musculature, cartilage, bones, and arteries. This important deficiency may lead to atherosclerosis. All tissue requires constant rebuilding to maintain proper function. Diminished growth hormone throughout life can lead to poor arterial repair and, eventually, heart disease. Growth hormone is also important for making

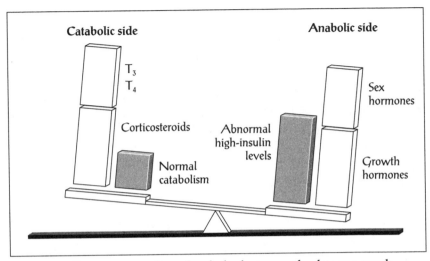

Figure 3.2 Overconsumption of carbohydrates can lead to too much insulin, and an imbalance in hormonal levels occurs.

new enzymes and other proteins in the body. If enzymes are not replaced, then the damage that naturally occurs during metabolism can have a negative effect on many cellular processes.

Growth hormone is not the only anabolic hormone that can diminish with excess carbohydrate consumption. The ability of the entire pituitary gland to produce its hormones is diminished. This is often observed in young boys by late onset of puberty and the belated growth of the sex organs. The reduction of carbohydrates in the diets of these boys often leads to rapid puberty because sex hormones get produced more when insulin levels decrease.

The continual consumption of carbohydrates may also explain why some people become less sexually active as they age. The more insulin they produce from overconsumption of carbohydrates, the lower the levels of the sex hormones. It's very possible that all that may be needed to increase one's sex drive is a reduction in carbohydrate consumption.

Besides the anabolic hormones, the catabolic hormones are also affected by too much insulin in the blood. The levels of the thyroid

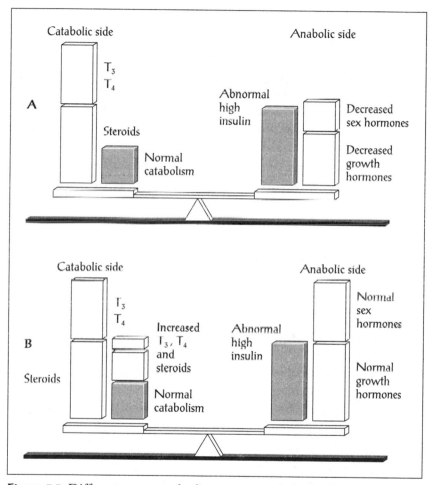

Figure 3.3 Different ways our bodies attempt to balance the increase of insulin from excess carbohydrate consumption: (A) decreases in other anabolic hormones; (B) increases in catabolic hormones.

hormones and corticosteroids are raised to compensate for the imbalance. These different possibilities are shown in Figure 3.3. Excessively high catabolic hormones can result in a weakened immune system and other problems, such as hyperthyroidism.

Now that we have shown that hormonal imbalance from excess carbohydrate consumption is the primary event that leads to many diseases, let's take a look at just what happens to people who have some hormonal imbalance. Many of us have experienced this imbalance—it is often associated with irritability and crankiness. Women experience these changes near their menstrual cycle. This is just one example of how imbalanced hormones can affect our daily lives. A more serious hormonal disease is diabetes, which we will focus on in chapter 4. This is such an important disease that we have devoted a whole chapter to it in this book. Let's take a look at some other metabolic imbalances associated with hormones.

GROWTH HORMONE DEFICIENCIES

Adults

We have touched upon the idea that increases in insulin can result in decreases in the production of growth hormone. When growth hormone was first discovered, it was thought to play a role only in the early years in life, mainly to control the body's growth from early childhood to adulthood. It eventually was shown that growth hormone is essential throughout a person's life.

Growth hormone deficiencies are common in people as they age, particularly people with adult-onset diabetes, another consequence of excess carbohydrate consumption. Too much insulin results in depressed levels of other anabolic hormones, such as growth hormone. Today in the United States, human growth hormone supplementation is approved for use in adults by the Food and Drug Administration. But is supplementation the only way to correct this problem?

Anyone who adopts a low-carbohydrate nutritional program for any appreciable length of time will notice many changes in her body that can be attributed partially to increases in growth hormone. Over time, fat is reduced and muscle begins to increase, even in the absence of exercise. With exercise, the increase in muscle is very rapid. Fingernails grow faster and hair growth responds as well. While one may not regain hair that is lost, usually the receding hairline stops. The rate of tissue repair and overall quality of the skin also improves.

Children

One of the great tragedies of our modern high-carbohydrate diets is that children suffer from insufficient fat and protein in their diet. Countless times we have observed very young children placed on low-fat diets. What do they eat? Carbohydrates—pasta, juice, cookies, cereal, candy, and low-fat milk. This is truly a sign that nutrition has taken a wrong turn. Growing bodies need protein and fat to make more tissue, and large amounts of growth hormone to send out the growth signals.

Recent work published in the journal *Pediatrics* sheds some light on how excess carbohydrate in the diets of children can reduce growth hormone production. The researchers, Melanie Smith, M.N.S., R.D., and Fima Lifshitz, M.D., from the department of Pediatrics at Maimonides Medical Center (Brooklyn, New York), studied the effects of fruit juice consumption, which is mostly sugar water with some vitamins, on children's growth. Smith and Lifshitz found that children fourteen to twenty-seven months old who had below normal growth patterns also consumed an excessive amount of fruit juice.[2] Some of the children also had a history of intestinal complaints and diarrhea. After nutritional intervention to supply more calories from fat and protein, weight gain increased to much higher levels, and the children began to thrive.

This research, and other papers published by Lifshitz, reveal the extent to which carbohydrates, in the form of fruit juice, can negatively influence development in children. This failure to thrive must extend into many organs and even the brain. A reduction in carbohydrate consumption is all that is required to correct the problem.

With the stage set for you to truly appreciate the remarkable benefit of reducing carbohydrates in your diet, we will now move on to discuss specific diseases that have been treated with carbohydrate restriction. In the next chapters, we will show you a lot of graphical data obtained by Dr. Lutz from his medical practice on several thousands of patients for over forty years. We urge you to take the time to look closely at this to become familiar with many areas of nutrition and health. After you read and understand this book, you will no longer accept the common dogma that there is no evidence that low-carbohydrate diets are beneficial. Moreover, you will have powerful evidence to the contrary at your fingertips.

CHAPTER FOUR

Diabetes and Insulin Resistance

MANY AGE-RELATED AND DEGENERATIVE diseases often accompany diabetes. The onset of diabetes and insulin resistance are actually the first physiological changes to take place before many other diseases begin to appear, such as cancer and heart disease. This is not a new idea. Many researchers and medical practitioners have found this to be true, and there are many studies besides Dr. Lutz's original work that indicate that insulin resistance and diabetes are the first signs that other metabolic disorders may follow.

As discussed earlier, insulin is the hormone responsible for responding to carbohydrates in the diet. Insulin is produced in the beta cells of the pancreas. The catabolic counterpart to insulin, glucagon, is produced in the alpha cells of the pancreas. Insulin plays a key role in diabetes because it is responsible for removing glucose from the blood and putting it into cells for energy or into the liver, muscle, and adipose tissue for storage as glycogen or fat.

In the big picture of health, a close inspection of many diseases indicates that insulin resistance is the first stage in a series of physiological imbalances that ultimately leads to cellular breakdown. Insulin resistance is a term given to a condition in which the body's ability to use glucose properly is diminished. There are various different levels of this, but, in essence, Type 2 diabetes is full-blown insulin resistance. The cause of insulin resistance may simply be too many carbohydrates in the diet over a long period of time. Eventually, in some individuals, the body develops insulin resistance as a countermeasure to excess insulin.

Today, with a decreased consumption of fat in the diet coupled with increased carbohydrates, diabetes and insulin resistance are at an all-time high. People are getting diabetes at an earlier age, as well. We venture to say that not one of you reading this book can look at the foods your children eat and say that they don't eat too many carbohydrates. We have been there ourselves! Breakfast cereals loaded with sugar and carbohydrates from grain; lunch sandwiches with only a thin slice of meat and maybe a bit of cheese between two slices of bread, along with potato chips, fruit, and a sweet for dessert (most lunches today are probably close to 90 percent carbohydrates); a fast-food supper that's mostly bun and fried potatoes or pizza crust with a sugar-water soda to wash it all down.

Diabetes is currently the only noninfectious disease designated by the World Health Organization as an epidemic. Estimates from the International Diabetes Federation and the American Diabetes Association are that more than fifteen million people in the United States have the adult form of diabetes, and at least one-hundred million people worldwide are afflicted with this form of the disease. But the numbers of people with a milder form of insulin resistance are probably much greater.

The bad news is that diabetes is clearly a disease of poor sugar metabolism, and sugar (i.e., carbohydrate) is the dietary source of this imbalance. The good news is that diabetes can be reversed by the reduction of carbohydrates in the diet. Of course, many people still argue that fat is the culprit. However, we will show that it boils down to eating too many carbohydrates; over and over again we have observed that a reduction of carbohydrates to 6 BUs (bread units) per day results in a dramatic benefit for people with diabetes. We feel certain that most adult diabetes could be prevented if the diet outlined in this book were followed before diabetes had the chance to begin.

As you will see throughout this book, insulin resistance has emerged as a unified theory to explain a primary physiological breakdown that results in a whole host of diseases. We think you will agree that the fat theory is no longer relevant.

When you eat any carbohydrate, your body responds by producing insulin to metabolize the sugar that results from the carbohydrate breakdown. This is a completely normal process. However, there are various abnormal ways that the body responds to an overload of carbohydrates.

TYPE 1 DIABETES

Type 1 diabetes, also called *juvenile diabetes*, is known in scientific terms as *insulin-dependent diabetes mellitus* (IDDM). It is a form of diabetes that appears very early in life when the ability of the pancreas to produce insulin is impaired. It is believed to be due to a viral infection that, along with the body's immune response, destroys the beta cells of the pancreas.

People with Type 1 diabetes must take daily injections of insulin. One of the great breakthroughs in drug development of modern times has been the production of recombinant human insulin. This has allowed for the large-scale manufacturing of this important compound, and has helped thousands of people lead relatively normal lives.

Individuals who have Type 1 diabetes must carefully monitor their blood glucose levels. Today this can be achieved using over-the-counter glucose strips and even newer devices, such as small handheld digital meters.

Our view of IDDM is that it is very similar to multiple sclerosis (MS) in that there is an initial infection most likely caused by a virus that is not quickly conquered by an immune system weakened from excess carbohydrate consumption. The immune system attacks not only the virus, but the tissue that was damaged by the virus. In IDDM, this tissue is the beta cells of the pancreas. In MS, it is the myelin nerve fiber tissue. In IDDM, the pancreatic beta cells are especially stressed from the constant production of insulin in a high-carbohydrate eater. The damaged tissue may begin to look foreign to the immune system, and eventually this will lead to well-known autoimmune responses. This point of view is not considered in current orthodox medicine, yet it fits the facts very well.

Let's look at this another way. Many of us have experienced a nagging cold or infection that just won't go away even when taking antibiotics. This is an example of autoaggression on tissue because of a weakened immune system. A strong immune system should fully eliminate common viruses and bacterial infections in a reasonable amount of time. We have found in these cases that medium doses of cortisone or prednisone (immunosuppressant drugs) for three to five days will eliminate the nagging symptoms from the initial infection.

How does this work? The prednisone or cortisone suppresses the immune system, which can be done safely if the virus has been subdued. They temporarily stop the autoaggression on the tissue. This allows for the tissue to heal, and when the therapy is discontinued, the immune system now recognizes the tissue as "self" and there are no more symptoms. When this does not work, then a full-blown autoimmune disease, such as juvenile diabetes or MS, sets in.

This is an ironic twist in the complicated world of the immune system. A weakened system from hormonal imbalances due to excess carbohydrate consumption actually leads to autoaggression of tissue because the initial event of an infection does not get dealt with rapidly enough.

TYPE 2 DIABETES

This form of diabetes is often called *adult-onset diabetes* because it usually develops later in life. The scientific term for Type 2 diabetes is *non-insulin-dependent diabetes mellitus* (NIDDM). This means that these people usually do not require insulin for their condition. This form afflicts the majority of diabetics—up to 90 percent of the total diagnosed cases.

SUGAR TESTS

There are three main tests that can be performed to evaluate whether the body is responding properly to sugar and if a person has a potential problem. One test measures the levels of sugar in the urine. The two others—the glucose tolerance test and fasting blood sugar test—measure blood levels.

Glucose Tolerance Test

This is the most helpful test used to evaluate a person's sugar metabolism. This test is a measurement of the body's tolerance to a dose of sugar. Here's how it works: A person is given an oral dose of glucose or some other sugar (usually dissolved in water). Blood is drawn at different time intervals after the glucose has been taken. Each blood sample is measured for the amount of glucose it contains. A graph is constructed to compare the time after the glucose was given and the blood glucose levels. This graph is called a glucose tolerance curve.

Let's look at one such graph. Figure 4.1 shows a typical glucose tolerance curve from a normal individual. The y-axis shows the blood levels of glucose in units called milligrams per deciliter (mg/dl). This is a concentration measurement. The x-axis is the time in hours.

It is important to understand this graph because it relates directly to insulin resistance and diabetes. You can see that there is a steep rise in the blood glucose level after drinking the glucose. This rise typically occurs after thirty to sixty minutes. This is what is expected because after a glucose load (a high-carbohydrate meal, for example), the glucose from the blood should be removed in various ways, depending on the particular needs of the individual, and if his system is working properly. The body either uses the glucose for energy by transporting it into different cells, or if energy requirements are met,

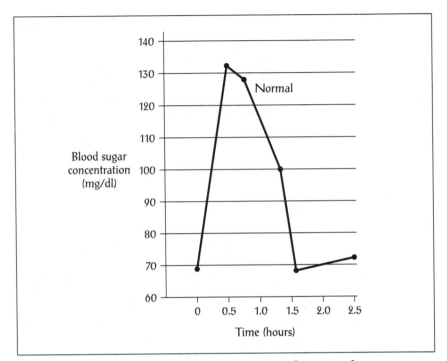

Figure 4.1 A glucose tolerance curve for a normal person after a sugar load of 50 grams of dextrose. There is a steep rise in blood glucose levels followed by a steady decline back to the normal initial level.

then the glucose is either stored in the liver as glycogen or in adipose tissue as triglycerides. Triglycerides are a form of fat, which, along with fatty acids, will be discussed in chapter 5.

You can see the trend in a normal individual shown in Figure 4.1. After about thirty minutes, the blood glucose levels began to decline. Starting levels (fasting) were reached at about one and one-half hours and then remained steady. This indicates that the body was able to handle the glucose it was supplied. But often this is not the case.

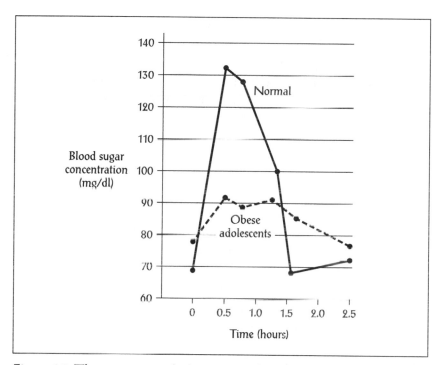

Figure 4.2 The steep curve depicts a normal reaction of the blood sugar to a single oral dose of 50 grams of dextrose (sugar). In overweight children a much flatter curve indicates that for the same stimulus, more insulin is produced. This overproduction of insulin (hyperinsulinemia) is the primary cause of "carbohydrate disease."

If you look at glucose tolerance curves of obese adolescents, you see a very different picture. Figure 4.2 shows what such a curve looks like, and we have added the "normal" curve to this graph to make it stand out.

The first thing you'll notice is that the increase in glucose in the blood is very much lower in obese adolescents as compared to normal people. A closer inspection reveals that fasting levels of blood glucose are higher. These are the levels at the beginning of the test or at the end.

Why do obese adolescents display this difference in the glucose tolerance curve? It's because they have a condition called hyperinsulinemia; their bodies produce too much insulin. Since insulin production is a direct response to eating carbohydrates, it seems logical that reducing carbohydrates would help to alleviate the excess production of insulin.

Here's the cycle we believe is taking place in these individuals: Large amounts of carbohydrates are consumed daily, causing a steady flow of insulin into the blood. This continues for years, getting to the point where more and more insulin is always in the blood. The pancreas, which produces insulin, is now very sensitive to any carbohydrate load. There is an overreaction by the pancreas, too much insulin is rapidly produced, and the glucose is removed from the blood too rapidly.

To make matters worse, the glucose is not fully utilized for energy and thus is stored as fat. This is a vicious cycle indeed. As more carbohydrates are eaten, more insulin is produced, and more fat is stored in adipose tissue.

Breaking the Vicious Cycle

Is it really as simple as reducing carbohydrate intake? Can this actually restore normal insulin metabolism? We feel the answer is "Yes!"

Let's examine the changes in glucose tolerance curves of obese adolescents after starting a low-carbohydrate diet. We have chosen to look at just seven patients to give you an idea of how their bodies adjust after reducing carbohydrates, but many more people have had the same result. These seven cases are shown in Figure 4.3.

In this figure, each patient's glucose tolerance curves are shown before starting a low-carbohydrate diet, and then after many months on a low-carbohydrate diet. These individuals consumed 6 or fewer BUs per day (72 grams of carbohydrates in twenty-four hours). In each case, there initially is a type of glucose tolerance curve similar to the one in Figure 4.2. This is the solid line in the figures. As you can see, there is not a large increase in blood sugar after a sugar load has been given.

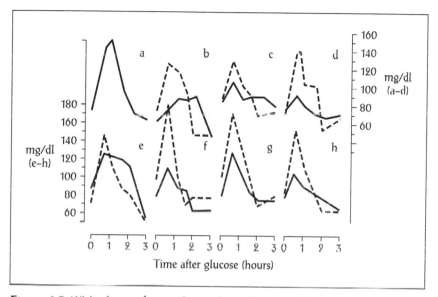

Figure 4.3 This shows the tendency for a glucose tolerance test in obese juveniles to return to normal on a low-carbohydrate diet consisting of 6 BUs per day. The lowercased "a" is a normal curve for comparison. Lowercased "b"–"h" are seven individual cases. The dotted lines are the curves after adopting the diet. Note the increase in height in the peak, which represents a reduction in hyperinsulinism.

The glucose tolerance curves for these same individuals after a few months on a low-carbohydrate diet are shown as a broken line in Figure 4.3. You can see a return to a more normal curve. There is a greater "spike" initially after ingesting the sugar, which shows that the pancreas is not overproducing insulin anymore, so there is a slower removal of glucose from the blood. Simply reducing their carbohydrate intake eliminated the hyperinsulinemia experienced by these adolescents—and no pills or potions were needed to achieve this desired result. Of course, the teenagers had to overcome their addiction to carbohydrates, which we concede is not always simple.

Hypoglycemia

There are other ways that diabetes can manifest itself. Many of us have experienced low blood sugar at one time or another. You probably assumed that this was fairly normal, and that a little food would solve the problem. This is not normal, but low blood sugar can virtually be eliminated by reducing your carbohydrate intake.

We realize that this idea goes against the concept that most doctors promote. They say if blood sugar is low, then eat more sugar and carbohydrates to raise it. Certainly in a moment of very low blood sugar, you would need some carbohydrate to remove the immediate problem, but this does nothing to put your body back into a normal insulin response situation.

As you shall see, too much carbohydrate in the diet is precisely the reason low blood sugar episodes occur. The process goes like this: Excessive consumption of carbohydrates leads to too much insulin release in the blood. In some people, this results in the constant removal of glucose from the blood, causing dangerously low levels of glucose. If sugar is consumed to help the condition, more insulin is produced and the low blood sugar episodes continue, often getting worse over time. Telling a patient, "If blood sugar is low, then eat more sugar and carbohydrates to raise it," is the same philosophy as telling drug addicts to keep taking that drug every time they go into withdrawal. In the long run, the drug addict should reduce the amount of drugs taken, until no more is being consumed and the episodes disappear.

To give you an idea of just what a hypoglycemic effect looks like, and how low-carbohydrate nutrition eliminates the problem, we have shown two glucose tolerance curves in Figure 4.4. The broken line is the glucose tolerance curve from one individual having low blood sugar episodes. This person was given 50 grams of glucose in tea, and then her blood glucose levels were measured over a six-hour period. Notice the drop to much lower levels of glucose after three hours (the broken line) compared to the solid line. This low drop is the hypoglycemic episode. It occurs in some people after they eat a mostly carbohydrate meal, usually after a few hours. To eliminate this problem, people usually find something to snack on, such as candy or bread, or perhaps some sugar in their coffee or tea. No one should have low blood sugar episodes just three or four hours after a meal, and we'll talk about this in more detail in the next chapter.

Now, let's get back to Figure 4.4. After just three months on a low-carbohydrate diet, this same patient no longer experienced hypoglycemic episodes. The glucose tolerance curve for this individual after carbohydrate restriction is shown as the solid line in Figure 4.4. Unlike before, there is no low blood sugar episode after three hours.

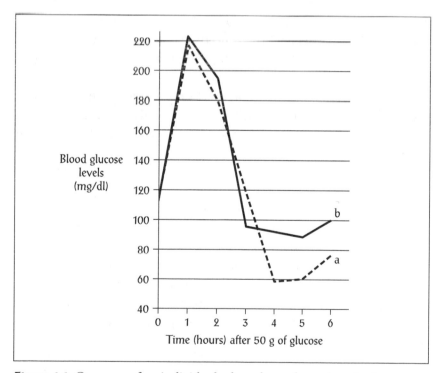

Figure 4.4 One case of an individual whose hypoglycemic episodes were eliminated after three months on a low-carbohydrate diet; (a) before the diet and (b) after the diet.

By reducing carbohydrate intake, insulin production becomes normal and too much sugar is not removed from the blood after a meal.

Remember, in the United States most of these people are told to eat more carbohydrates, not fewer. But as you have seen, this only adds to the problem. So, the next time your doctor tells you to eat more carbohydrates to eliminate low blood sugar episodes, ask to see the glucose tolerance curves of patients who have been treated successfully by a high-carbohydrate diet.

Fasting Blood Sugar

The fasting blood sugar test is what most people have when they get a physical. It's easier than a glucose tolerance test because only one sample of blood is needed. It has no time course, and in our opinion is not as informative as a glucose tolerance test, but it does give some indication of blood sugar regulation.

The test simply measures the level of glucose in the blood after fasting for some defined period of time, usually overnight without breakfast. Normal individuals have relatively low levels of glucose (70 to 90) when fasting. The numbers vary, but when the number goes beyond 100, it definitely signals that something is wrong.

The Problem with High Glucose Levels

Why is it so damaging to the body when glucose levels are elevated in the blood? The answer to this question lies in the chemistry and biochemistry of glucose and its interactions with proteins and lipids.

Proteins are large molecules that make up a large part of the functional biochemical reactions in your body. Among the most important are the enzymes. Enzymes are proteins that catalyze, or speed up, biochemical reactions. Without enzymes, all of the chemical reactions in animals (and all life-forms) would take too long to be useful to sustain life.

One of the main problems associated with too much glucose in the blood and tissues is that glucose can react chemically with proteins and destroy their ability to function. These reactions—called *glycation reactions*—don't need enzymes to take place. The only requirements are that the protein and glucose molecules must collide with each other, and there must be enough energy for the reaction to take place once they collide. (There are other requirements, based on rules of organic chemistry, but they're not important to understand for this purpose.)

As in all nonenzymatic chemical reactions, the higher the concentration of the two species that are reacting, the faster they will react. Also, more reactions will take place if concentrations are higher. Thus, high levels of glucose in the blood create more of these harmful glycation reactions.

Sugars that react in this way, such as glucose, are called *reducing sugars*. They also can react with lipids (fats) that make up cellular membranes. The higher the levels of these sugars in our blood and tissues, the greater the chance that the destructive reactions between proteins, lipids, and reducing sugars will take place. The process eventually can lead to the destruction of cellular function. Thus, it is very important to keep sugar levels in the blood at relatively low levels throughout your life. As you saw from the various glucose tolerance curves presented earlier, it is normal for the sugar level to rise when a glucose load is given, but it should be removed from the blood within a few hours. The proper balance of sugar metabolism is what is needed to maintain good health. If you are continually snacking on carbohydrate foods, then sugar levels in the blood are always elevated.

Physicians use a test to determine how bad the glycation reactions are in your system if you have diabetes. In this test, the blood protein called *hemoglobin*, which carries oxygen to tissues, is measured for the amount of sugar that is bound to it. The more sugar, the worse the diabetes. There are many proteins in mammals that have carbohydrates bound to them, and these are required for some bodily functions. But these proteins are made and the carbohydrate is added to the protein using the cellular machinery. The reaction of proteins indiscriminately with glucose is not controlled, and not biologically required. It is a detrimental effect because it can stop a protein or enzyme from functioning properly.

If it's so important to keep sugar levels reasonably low throughout one's lifetime, then how can one do it? Despite how simple our answer is, there is still much resistance to the solution.

EAT LESS CARBOHYDRATE

If your sugar levels are too high, then eat less sugar. It's that simple. Drugs to lower glucose levels in diabetics are prescribed by physicians and heavily promoted by pharmaceutical companies. Diabetic patients are often told that their dietary control starts with their fat intake; carbohydrates are discussed, but there is usually no recommendation to reduce carbohydrate levels.

Type 2 diabetes is a disease of carbohydrate overload. By eating carbohydrates in quantities that humans, as hunters and gatherers, did not evolve to eat, people simply have overwhelmed their bodies' natural ability to process these sugars. How can a physician say that you have too much glucose in your blood, but that you don't have to worry about how much sugar you eat? This is both preposterous and dangerous. Don't be fooled by those who insist that reducing carbohydrate intake will not help diabetics.

As with almost everything in life, excess will lead to some negative process. If you're a baseball pitcher, eventually your arm cannot keep up with the demand, which is why pitchers are rotated every three or four games. If you drink gin, your liver may be unable to metabolize the alcohol after a period of years. If you smoke too many cigarettes, at some point your lungs and body will no longer be able to remove the toxic by-products. Obviously this list could go on and on.

In our experience, almost everyone benefits from carbohydrate restriction, even if they have had Type 2 diabetes for years and are taking drugs to lower their glucose levels. In Figure 4.5, we show the change in the average fasting blood sugar levels of fifteen pa-

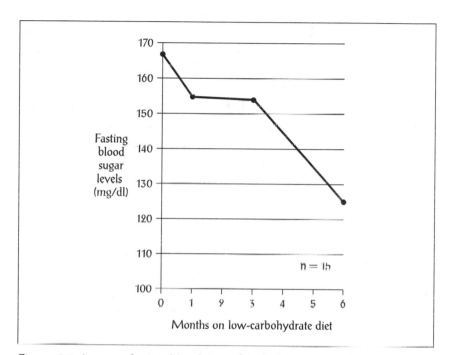

Figure 4.5 Average fasting blood sugar levels for fifteen patients with slight diabetes after six months with a diet of 72 g of carbohydrates. The average value dropped from 165 to 127 mg/dl.

tients after six months on a diet consisting of 72 grams of carbohydrates or less per day. These patients had been on glucose-lowering drugs when they began the diet. After six months, the average levels dropped from 165 mg/dl to 127 mg/dl. In addition, fewer of the glucose-lowering drugs were needed. This is more direct evidence that reducing carbohydrates will reduce blood sugar levels.

When one author, Dr. Allan, was working at the National Institutes of Health, he presented a colleague, Dr. Dolph Hatfield, with the information you have just read about. Hatfield is elderly and has Type 2 diabetes, but he is still a very active man. He began the low-carbohydrate diet because it made sense to him. After less than six months on the diet, Hatfield has become a believer. He has reported that even though he has decreased his glucose-lowering pharmaceuticals in half, his blood glucose levels have dropped significantly. The measurement of glycated hemoglobin is also much improved. Furthermore, Hatfield has said that he no longer experiences low blood sugar episodes and is less tired. He even told us that it is the complex carbohydrates, the ones that you are always told to eat, that cause the greatest low blood sugar episodes. Many people will say this is anecdotal evidence, but it is very real to Dolph Hatfield, just as it can be for you.

It's important for diabetic patients to note a few things about the transition to a low-carbohydrate diet.

First, as with any physical problem, you should be in constant communication with your physician. Don't let him dissuade you from going on a low-carbohydrate diet, but do make sure he monitors the progress. It will be a learning experience for both of you—perhaps in this way more and more medical practitioners can learn the true benefit of carbohydrate restriction.

Second, remember that it takes time for the body to adjust and to correct physical imbalances that took years to occur. All too often people expect instant results, but time is necessary. As you will note in later chapters, some individuals with certain metabolic disorders required years on a low-carbohydrate diet to achieve optimal health, but achieve it they did! There are a few diseases where little is known about the effects of carbohydrate restriction, and these will be discussed later.

You can see from what we have presented so far that most people benefit from a reduction of carbohydrates, especially when following the diet as outlined in chapters 2 and 12 in this book. This is also true for those who suffer from one of the metabolic problems we have discussed, or those who wish to reduce their risk of getting diabetes later in life. This means that virtually everyone can benefit from this program. However, we would like to reassure you that this is not a fad diet, but rather, it is the diet that our physiology has evolved into. The true fad diet of today is, in fact, eating too many carbohydrates. This fact will be reinforced throughout this book, particularly in chapter 11 when we explore evolution.

NEW STUDIES, OLD SOLUTIONS

A literature search using the National Library of Medicine's on-line search tool reveals that numerous studies with carbohydrate restriction have been performed recently. One study performed at the University of California, Irvine, Medical Center, at the Department of Obstetrics and Gynecology, looked at the effects of carbohydrate restriction in patients with diet controlled gestational diabetes mellitus (GDM).[1]

Often during pregnancy there is a short-term development of diabetes and insulin resistance. These studies were designed to look at the effects of carbohydrates on various measurable factors related to sugar metabolism that are known to be important during pregnancy. Two groups of women were assigned randomly to either the high-carbohydrate group (daily carbohydrate exceeding 45 percent of total calories) or the low-carbohydrate group (daily carbohydrate below 42 percent of total calories).

The conclusions from these experiments were "carbohydrate restriction in patients with diet-controlled GDM results in improved glycemic control, less need for insulin therapy, a decrease in the incidence of large-for-gestational-age infants, and a decrease in cesarean deliveries." To clarify, "improved glycemic control" means that the women's metabolism of sugar worked better, thus there was less need for prescribed insulin treatments. The size of the fetus was more normal in carbohydrate-restricted pregnant women; and there were more normal deliveries, as opposed to the need for cesarean section deliveries.

This experiment with pregnant women shows several distinct and important benefits of low-carbohydrate nutrition. As with many low-carbohydrate experiments performed throughout the world, the levels of carbohydrates used in these studies are much higher than we propose. A diet consisting of 6 BUs per day amounts to about 10 to 15 percent of one's daily calories from carbohydrates. Nonetheless, even at less than 42 percent of total calories, the researchers observed a decrease in insulin resistance and also a decrease in cesarean deliveries. We would expect, based on all the evidence we present in this book, that pregnant women will benefit even more from a 6 BUs per day low-carbohydrate program, and so will their babies.

In another set of experiments, the effects of carbohydrate in people with newly diagnosed Type 2 diabetes was explored. In this work, researchers looked at abnormal lipoprotein in these diabetics.[2] Lipoproteins are proteins involved in the transport of lipids (fats). Some lipoproteins move cholesterol, a very important biomolecule, to various parts of the body. You may know some of them as HDL (high-density lipoprotein) and LDL (low-density lipoprotein), but there are others. A more detailed look at these can be found in chapter 6.

Diabetics have an abnormality in their fat metabolism because of the abnormality in their sugar metabolism—the two are closely related. In simple terms, if sugar and insulin levels are high, then fat is stored and not used. It is only when carbohydrates are reduced that fat can be mobilized.

The researchers looked at hyperlipoproteinemia in diabetic patients. Hyperlipoproteinemia means too many lipoproteins in the blood. In diabetics, this arises because of the same old problem: too much insulin, which places the body on anabolic overload and promotes the storage of fat. Since lipoproteins are associated with fat transport, they increase in numbers because the body is attempting to find a place to store fat. *Keep in mind that fat intake is not the problem. If carbohydrates are reduced, then fat is metabolized and lipoprotein numbers would normalize.*

Initially, forty-two patients were placed on a low-carbohydrate diet. Of these forty-two, 57 percent had hyperlipoproteinemia. After only one month on a low-carbohydrate diet, half of the 57 percent with hyperlipoproteinemia reverted to normal. After ten months, only eight diabetics still had high lipoprotein levels. This represents a 66 percent success rate in only ten months! The authors conclude that "the common lipoprotein abnormalities of maturity-onset diabetes can usually be returned to normal by the simplest possible carbohydrate-restricted diet. Specialized and complex diets or lipid-lowering drugs are unnecessary in the majority of patients."

Are you starting to see the power in low-carbohydrate nutrition? Since it's evident that lowering carbohydrate intake actually can reverse many metabolic abnormalities, you can also conclude that such conditions could be stopped from developing altogether if the diet were used throughout a lifetime.

There are many more studies that reveal the benefit of low-carbohydrate nutrition; however, there are also many that suggest that low-carbohydrate nutrition is unhealthy. In all of the studies we have seen, the carbohydrate is either not low enough to test the diet we outline, or the amount of time that people were studied was too short. As we mentioned before, and as we shall see later, some conditions require a rather long time to benefit from low-carbohydrate nutrition.

Dr. Gerald Reaven is one well-known researcher who has been outspoken in linking insulin resistance to degenerative diseases. Reaven is one of the first people in the United States to propose that insulin resistance is the key to various metabolic diseases associated with aging and degeneration. At Stanford University, Reaven and his colleagues have performed many well-designed studies over the last twenty years that tend to support the low-carbohydrate nutritional program, even though Reaven focuses primarily on weight loss.

One of the greatest myths going today is that you cannot become fat from eating carbohydrates. Yet the production of triglycerides, the form of fat that gets stored in adipose tissue, is a result of excess carbohydrate consumption. If carbohydrates are not used immediately for energy, they are converted by biochemical reactions into triglycerides, or into glycogen. It doesn't take much to fill up the body's glycogen storage bank, so triglycerides are produced from glucose and other sugars. As many of you know, this is where most of the sugar goes. Triglycerides are associated with numerous problems, heart disease being the most predominant.

Reaven and his coworkers have shown in numerous human studies that triglycerides do result from carbohydrate consumption, and that other metabolic problems such as high blood pressure and increased risk for heart disease are associated with insulin resistance.

One such study was published in 1989.[3] In this study, patients with adult-onset diabetes were placed on two different diets. One diet consisted of 60 percent carbohydrate and 20 percent fat, and the other consisted of 40 percent carbohydrate and 40 percent fat. In the higher carbohydrate group, it was found that total blood insulin levels and glucose levels were significantly elevated throughout the day. Glucose excretion in the urine in a twenty-four-hour period doubled for the high-carbohydrate group, and fasting triglyceride levels also increased by more than 30 percent. As with everything we have shown up to now, it was the carbohydrates in the diet, not the fat, that caused most of the problems.

Also in 1989, an editorial by Reaven et al. in the journal *Diabetes Care* suggests that a recent trend to allow more sucrose consumption in the diets of diabetics is not such a wise idea.[4] They support this opinion with the fact that many studies show high-carbohydrate diets are correlated with hyperglycemia, hyperinsulinemia, hypertriglyceridemia, and hypercholesterolemia. These are all medical terms for too much glucose, insulin, triglycerides, and cholesterol, respectively. The researchers mention that these results are documented from many well-controlled prospective studies. They do concede that some studies disagree, but they point out that this does not necessarily prove supportive studies to be incorrect.

Many more studies from Reaven's research group have been published over the years; many of these explain how all the conditions that give rise to diabetes also affect heart disease parameters. Chapter 6 will explore some of these studies in more detail.

Let's consider one more study that provides evidence that high-carbohydrate diets are not conducive to good health. Eight patients with Type 2 diabetes were fed either a diet that contained 15 percent protein, 40 percent fat, and 45 percent carbohydrate, or a diet that contained 15 percent protein, 25 percent fat, and 60 percent carbohydrate.[5] The research in this study focused on heart disease parameters. Researchers found that replacing saturated fat with carbohydrate resulted in an increase in triglycerides, and therefore an increased risk for coronary artery disease. The study authors conclude: "Since triglyceride-rich lipoproteins may be atherogenic, appropriate dietary advice for patients with Type 2 diabetes may deserve reappraisal."

What they're really saying is that cardiologists should stop telling patients that a low-fat, high-carbohydrate diet is healthy, when studies show quite the opposite, and furthermore these physicians should tell patients that this type of diet is particularly bad for people with existing Type 2 diabetes.

As we have already shown you, the results from Dr. Lutz's years of clinical observations show that a reduction of carbohydrates to about 72 grams per day will result in elimination of insulin resistance. The 40 to 45 percent carbohydrate numbers used in the other cited studies are still too high to see the full benefit, and Reaven's studies were not designed to follow patients for a long period of time to see if their sugar metabolism normalizes.

In spite of everything we have presented in this chapter and throughout the book, you are still going to run into the same old myth that low-fat diets and high-carbohydrate foods are the "healthy" choice. Certainly the American government agencies' line of thinking in these areas has not changed, even though ample evidence exists to denounce the low-fat theory.

CHAPTER FIVE

Energy: Less Is More

ENERGY IS A TOPIC THAT CONCERNS us all, every day in every way. Whether you are trying to get the kids off to school or running a marathon, energy is the buzzword that all of us can relate to.

Most of us think of energy in terms of how we feel: "Am I tired?" "Do I have enough energy to finish mowing the lawn, or to make dinner?" Our overall well-being and ability to perform tasks is our individual measure of energy. But what is energy, and how is it created inside our body and in our cells?

These questions are so fundamentally important that we are devoting an entire chapter to discussing them. There are a great many myths surrounding energy production in the body and which foods supply energy. We hope to dispel some of the common themes that surround the dogma regarding carbohydrates and energy.

The most popular refrain for eating large amounts of carbohydrates is that people must consume them in their diet to get energy. Not only is this statement inaccurate, it also is misleading. The body has very specific mechanisms for generating energy. Using carbohydrates is only one such mechanism, and not necessarily the best one.

Furthermore, you do not need to eat carbohydrates to have them available for energy. Your body can make carbohydrates as needed, if the protein supply is adequate. Reducing your daily intake of carbohydrates to 72 grams or less—6 bread units—will result in *more* energy at your disposal, *as long as you eat plenty of fat and protein.* Don't just take our word for it: Try it for yourself! Only by direct experience will you appreciate the effects of low-carbohydrate nutrition on your own energy levels.

This chapter is one of the more technical chapters in this book. It may require reading more than once. Our purpose is to dispel some of the many inaccurate statements and old wives' tales that surround the physiology of energy production in people. Carbohydrates are *not* required to obtain energy. Fat supplies more energy than a comparable amount of carbohydrate, and low-carbohydrate diets tend to make your system of producing energy more efficient. Furthermore, many organs prefer fat for energy.

Here is a little tidbit that should shake you up. We have all been led to believe that low-fat diets are heart-healthy. But did you know that your heart primarily uses fat for energy? That's right. Carbohydrates contribute very little to the energy necessary to keep your heart beating, and the preferred fat is saturated fat. Thus, if you eat a high-carbohydrate diet, you are depriving your heart of exactly what it prefers to keep it beating.

If you are not interested in the specific biochemistry of energy production, then you could skip this chapter without losing the main point of the book. We will, however, use some of the principles from this chapter in chapter 10, so we recommend you at least glance through this material. But if you skip this chapter, you will need to accept our point that you do not need carbohydrates to get energy, even the much-touted fast energy.

ENERGY CYCLES

Energy production is a fundamental process required for life. It entails much more than simply having enough energy to walk up the stairs; without proper energy production, your cells cannot divide, all of the biochemical reactions that allow you to function will dissipate, and your body, as an organism, eventually will cease to function.

Energy can exist in many forms, such as heat, light, electrical, and chemical energy, but one of the basic laws of physics stipulates that energy cannot be created or destroyed. It can only be changed from one form to another, and this is how it works for life on Earth.

The overall energy cycle of life is derived from the sun. The sun supplies the initial energy from nuclear fusion reactions that make animal and plant life possible.

Sunlight, one form of energy, gets converted by plants, trees, and shrubs into carbohydrates and oxygen. This process is called *photo-synthesis*. Besides sunlight, photosynthesis also requires carbon diox ide and water. Melvin Calvin and scientists who worked with him during the 1950s at the University of California at Berkeley determined the many chemical steps that were involved in photosynthesis. Calvin was awarded the Nobel Prize in chemistry in 1961 for his achievements in this area, and now photosynthesis is often called the Calvin cycle.

After making carbohydrates, animals consume the plants, and they use the breakdown of carbohydrates for energy. Carbohydrates also can be stored in animals as fat, which can be used by the other animals who eat them for energy. One by-product from the breakdown of carbohydrates is carbon dioxide, which the animals release into the environment, to be used by plants for photosynthesis. This, then, is the basic energy cycle.

In between the simple steps we just discussed there are many important steps that take place. In the course of this chapter, we want you to become familiar with how animals produce energy, as well as how animal energy production is different from primitive cell organisms. In turn, this information will help to dispel the myths surrounding carbohydrates and energy.

THE ENERGY OF LIFE

The energy used to support life is in the form of chemical energy that, as we have said, begins with the sun. This chemical energy arises from two basic processes. In one process, a molecule that supplies energy—food, for example—is oxidized to release energy. In another process, energy is obtained by rearrangement of molecules without oxidation.

Oxidation is a process that removes electrons (negatively charged subatomic particles) or adds oxygen to a molecule. The electrons that are removed from a food molecule are used by some cells to make energy. This process requires oxygen. In other types of cells, a process called *fermentation* takes place. Fermentation is a series of chemical steps that also yield energy, but this happens in the absence of oxygen, so no overall oxidation takes place.

In both of these processes, a molecule is generated called *adenosine triphosphate*, or ATP. This is the molecule that has the stored energy in the form of chemical bonds. Figure 5.1 shows the chemical structure of ATP. There are three phosphate groups (triphosphate) bound to an adenosine group. The important parts of this molecule are the phosphate groups because this is where the chemical energy is stored.

When cells need energy for their many different functions, the ATP molecule serves as the supplier by releasing the chemical energy stored within its chemical bonds. However, in order to release

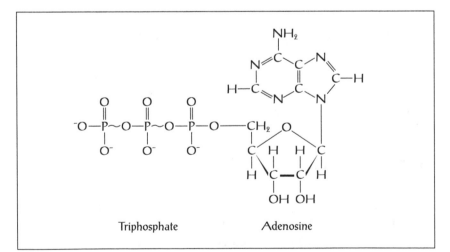

Figure 5.1 The chemical structure of ATP (adenosine triphosphate), the main molecule that supplies cellular energy.

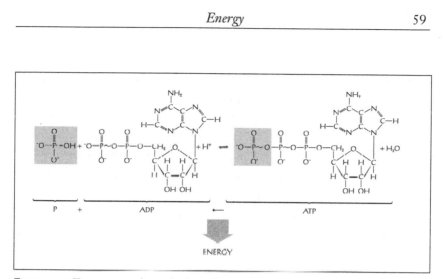

Figure 5.2 Energy is released when the ATP molecule gets broken by water into ADP and P. The bond breakage occurs at the shaded phosphate.

this energy for cells to use, the bonds must be broken. Two new molecules result from the bond breakage of ATP. These two new molecules are called *adenosine diphosphate* (ADP) and *phosphate* (P). By breaking one of the phosphate bonds, energy is released. This general process is summarized in Figure 5.2. In contrast, the stored energy in food is required to make ATP. This is another energy cycle of life.

The steps involved in making, storing, and using energy require an initial energy source. In the case of animals, this energy source is food. The food molecules get oxidized in the body's cells in order to release electrons from them. These electrons are used to make the ATP molecule, and in turn ATP is used by cells for energy. This is another of the many cycles that take place in life.

It is important to know:

- how different organisms obtain energy
- which food molecules are best for different organisms
- what the requirements are for different tissues and organs for the more complicated organisms

So many people believe, without scientific proof, that carbohydrates are what we need for energy, and that eating more carbohydrates will give us more energy. Yet, most of us have had experiences that suggest this isn't true. That sugary afternoon snack comes to mind—afterward you don't feel so great because energy levels usually decrease after the initial "rush." This is a direct result of low blood sugar from the overproduction of insulin.

So let's take a look at how different organisms create energy, and find out just how important carbohydrates are to humans.

CELLS: PAST AND PRESENT

The Earth is approximately four and a half billion years old. In all that time, only two different cell types have evolved: prokaryotes and eukaryotes. Bacteria were the first cells to live on this planet, and they are the prokaryotes. Higher life-forms marked the beginning of eukaryotic cell development, and eukaryotic cells make up the cells in all animals.

The main difference between these two cell types is that eukaryotes have cellular organelles, and prokaryotes don't. (You may recall the term *organelle* from biology class. Some representative organelles are the nucleus, ribosome, golgi apparatus, and mitochondria.) Organelles are specialized compartments within eukaryotic cells; they have specific functions and are surrounded by semipermeable membranes to isolate them from other parts of the cell.

Prokaryotes are much simpler than eukaryotes. In prokaryotic cells, there are no specialized organelles. All of the biochemical functions required to sustain life take place inside the cell in a kind of "cell soup," and there is no separation of different components.

The differences between these two types of cells are important because they give us clues about energy production in humans and how that differs from bacterial cell energy production. There also are some important differences in how these types of cells produce energy to sustain life.

ENERGY PRODUCTION IN PROKARYOTIC CELLS

We hope readers are still with us! This background information is essential for understanding the production of energy in human cells and because it relates to many aspects of cancer that will be presented in chapter 10.

Since bacteria, or prokaryotes, appeared on Earth before oxygen was available, they had to produce energy in the absence of oxygen. This is the process of fermentation. Any process that takes place in the absence of oxygen is called an anaerobic process.

Bacteria mainly use glucose as their energy source. Glucose is a six-carbon molecule. The biochemical steps related to breaking down glucose to obtain energy are called glycolysis. The word *glycolysis* comes from the Greek roots *glycos*, meaning "sweet," and *lysis*, meaning "loosening," so glycolysis literally means "the loosening or splitting of something sweet."

The accepted view throughout the biochemical and biological scientific literature is that glycolysis is a primitive process, thought to have begun very early in biological history, before cells evolved to have specialized organelles. However, glycolysis remains a very important aspect of energy production in advanced life-forms, and occurs in almost every living cell. Most of the decisive work in discovering the glycolytic pathways was done in the 1930s by the German biochemists G. Embden, O. Meyerhof, and O. Warburg.

Remember how energy production involves making ATP to be used throughout the cell? The basic steps in turning glucose into ATP involve the splitting, or breakdown, of the glucose molecule into two new molecules, each containing three carbons. One of the products of this breakdown is called glyceraldehyde-3-phosphate. Glyceraldehyde-3-phosphate is the only product from the glucose breakdown that can be oxidized; hence, its metabolism is the key to understanding how ATP is generated from glucose.

Here's how it works: After glyceraldehyde-3-phosphate is formed, a series of metabolic steps involving numerous enzymes convert it into phosphoenol pyruvate (PEP). The phosphate group is removed from PEP at this point to yield another very important molecule, called *pyruvate*. This is the exact step where ATP is generated from the original glycolysis of glucose. At this stage, two ATP molecules are generated for every one glucose molecule that was broken down because there are two PEP molecules for every glucose molecule. The ATP molecules can now be used for different energy purposes inside the cells.

There are many more biochemical steps in glycolysis that are known to occur, but they are beyond the scope of this book. Still, it's important to at least have a feel for what takes place inside the cell.

Back to pyruvate. This three-carbon molecule has various fates, depending upon what type of cell it's from and what energy needs the cell has.

In one anaerobic reaction, pyruvate gets converted to the molecule lactate. Lactate is an end product of the anaerobic oxidation of glucose. You may already have heard of lactic acid—it's a by-product that builds up in muscle tissue during strenuous exercise. This occurs because when depleted of oxygen, the cells in muscle tissue begin to make energy anaerobically, just like the cells of bacteria, and they produce lactic acid as the by-product.

The breakdown of glucose to lactate is only one type of fermentation, but it happens to be the simplest chemical fermentation that is known, which is consistent with its designation as a very primitive process.

Another type of fermentation is one that produces ethyl alcohol, otherwise known as the alcohol that you drink. In this process, the six-carbon glucose molecule is broken down to a two-carbon molecule, ethyl alcohol, and a one-carbon molecule, carbon dioxide (CO_2). Two ethyl alcohol and two carbon dioxide molecules are formed from every one-glucose molecule. Yeast are the organisms that are used to make the fermentation products that many of us enjoy from time to time. Yeast are among the simplest eukaryotic organisms, and are actually very interesting. One of the reasons yeast use fermentation is for survival. In an overripe piece of fruit, for example, yeast will ferment the sugar deep within the fruit where there is little oxygen, which will generate alcohol. The alcohol kills any bacteria that are present, but the yeast survive. Once the yeast are exposed to oxygen after the fruit decomposes, the yeast can switch and use the alcohol for energy. They're very clever little organisms!

ENERGY PRODUCTION IN EUKARYOTIC CELLS

As time progressed on Earth, plants eventually emerged and began to produce oxygen as a by-product of their metabolism. Other organisms then adapted to the presence of oxygen, and a major change was made in the way that energy was produced. Oxygen became the fuel that drives the generation of ATP. Respiration is the name given to the process of obtaining energy in the presence of oxygen.

Everyone knows that we need oxygen to live. This is because oxygen is used by the body's cells to produce energy by aerobic oxidation. Eukaryotes produce energy in the cellular organelles called the *mitochondria. The mitochondria are perhaps the most important organelles in our bodies because they generate almost all of the energy we need to survive. Without them, our cells could not support life.*

The proper function of the mitochondria is critical to human health, and carbohydrates and fat play key roles in mitochondrial metabolism. Now we will reveal just how cells produce energy and why carbohydrates are not required as a specific dietary factor in energy production. We will also take a look at different organs and what their energy needs are. We hope you're beginning to see that there's much more to the story of energy in your body than simply the idea that you need plenty of carbohydrates for fuel.

RESPIRATION AND MITOCHONDRIA

The process of respiration, that is, using oxygen to generate energy, appeared on the Earth after oxygen became available. Oxygen has the chemical ability to remove electrons from other molecules.

After the atmosphere on Earth became concentrated with oxygen, cells evolved to use this as a source of oxidation instead of using the fermentation pathway. Eukaryotic cells, present in organisms more complex than bacteria, emerged from these changes. Along with the formation of eukaryotic cells came the evolutionary breakthrough known as the mitochondria.

Mitochondria are the power plants of the cell. Because they produce most of the energy in the body, the amount of energy available is based on how well the mitochondria are working. Whenever you think of energy, think of all those mitochondria churning out ATP to make the entire body function correctly. The amount of mitochondria in each cell varies, but up to 50 percent of the total cell volume can be mitochondria. When you get tired, don't just assume you need more carbohydrates; instead, think in terms of how you can maximize your mitochondrial energy production through respiration.

INSIDE THE MITOCHONDRIA

If you could shrink to a small enough size to get inside the mitochondria, what would you discover? The first thing you'd learn is that the mitochondria are primarily designed to use fat for energy! This is a very important point that we need to examine further.

Mitochondria were specifically designed to use fat for energy.

ATP from the Mitochondria

The complete steps in making ATP within mitochondria are numerous and very complicated, but a look at the five major parts of ATP production will be all that is needed for you to know how energy is created in our cells. These five steps are summarized in Exhibit 5.1. Each step is discussed in more detail below. Don't get

---

Exhibit 5.1

The five major steps in producing ATP within the mitochondria

Step 1 Fuel source transported into mitochondria
Step 2 Fuel converted into acetyl-CoA
Step 3 Oxidation of acetyl-CoA to remove electrons
Step 4 Electrons transported through electron transport chain
           (or respiratory chain)
Step 5 Oxidative phosphorylation to produce ATP

---

bogged down with the scientific names. Just go with it for a while and you will see how it all fits together. Remember that these chemical steps are taking place thousands of times per second all over your body.

Step 1: Transportation of a Fuel Source into the Mitochondria

Since the process of making ATP actually takes place inside the mitochondria, the necessary fuel must first be transported there. The fuel is either derived from glucose or from fatty acids. Fatty acids are the chemical name for fat. They have a charged acidic group on the end of them, which is why they are called fatty acids. Fatty acids can be saturated or unsaturated.

Fatty acids are transported into the mitochondria completely intact. L-carnitine is the compound necessary to transport medium- and large-sized fatty acids inside the mitochondria from the cell soup (called *cytosol*). Think of L-carnitine as a subway train that brings people into the city from the suburbs; likewise, L-carnitine brings fats into the mitochondria. L-carnitine is chiefly found in animal products. (Its name is derived from the Greek word *carnis*, meaning "meat" or "flesh.") L-carnitine is one of many very important substances that are only found in appreciable quantities in animal foods, which is another reason to eat foods derived from animals. We will discuss more of these substances throughout the book, particularly in the chapter on vitamins and minerals.

Once inside our cells, glucose gets broken down by the process of glycolysis, just as in bacteria. This breakdown takes place outside the mitochondria. Two possibilities may now occur. The product from glycolysis (pyruvate) can either move into the mitochondria to be oxidized, or it can be broken down to lactate outside the mitochondria by a fermentative process similar to the one described for bacteria.

To summarize this step: Fat is transported into the mitochondria as a complete, intact molecule. Glucose gets broken down outside the mitochondria, and the product of this glycolysis (pyruvate) either gets transported into the mitochondria, or it is used anaerobically to produce energy and the by-product lactate.

Step 2: Fuel Is Converted into Acetyl-CoA
After the fatty acids are inside the mitochondria, they are oxidized by a process called *beta-oxidation*. Remember: Oxidation means that electrons are removed from a molecule. In the beta-oxidation process, fats are broken down into two carbon molecules. This process releases electrons to be used in step two. Acetyl-CoA is the direct product from beta-oxidation of fats inside the mitochondria. When pyruvate enters the mitochondria from glycolysis, it must be converted into acetyl-CoA by an enzyme reaction. Acetyl-CoA is the starting point for the next cycle in the production of ATP inside the mitochondria.

Step 3: Oxidation of Acetyl-CoA and the TCA Cycle
The cycle that oxidizes the acetyl-CoA is called the TCA (tricarboxylic acid) cycle. Electrons are removed from acetyl-CoA, and carbon dioxide (CO_2) is generated as a by-product. Carbon dioxide is the oxidized product of acetyl-CoA. Carbon dioxide is the by-product of mitochondrial respiration, and is eliminated from our bodies through our breathing or through our skin.

Step 4: Electrons Are Transported Through the Respiratory Chain
The electrons obtained from the oxidation of acetyl-CoA, which ultimately came from fats or sugar, are shuttled through many molecules as part of the electron transport chain inside the mitochondria.
Some of the molecules are proteins, while others are small, non-
protein cofactor molecules. One of these cofactor molecules is another important substance that is mainly found in animal foods. It is
called *coenzyme Q-10*. Without coenzyme Q-10, mitochondrial respiration would be unable to function, and energy production would
be minimal.

Step four also is the step where oxygen comes into play. Oxygen
accepts the electrons at this stage and is then chemically reduced to
water.

Step 5: Oxidative Phosphorylation
As electrons travel down the electron transport chain, they cause
electrical fluctuations between the inner and outer membrane in the
mitochondria. These chemical gradients, as they are sometimes
called, are the driving force that produces ATP in the process called
oxidative phosphorylation. ATP is made from ADP and a phosphate
molecule (the reverse of its breakdown for energy), just like in bacteria. The ATP is transported outside the mitochodria for the cell to
use as energy for any of its thousands of biochemical reactions.

These five steps are summarized in Figure 5.3.

WHAT DOES IT ALL MEAN, ANYWAY?

During their evolution, cells developed an organelle that specifically uses fat for energy. This suggests that using fat metabolism for
energy production is part of a higher form of life. If there were no
mitochondria, then fat metabolism for energy would be limited and
not very efficient. Bacteria are able to use some fat for energy, but
they prefer glucose and other easily oxidized carbon sources.

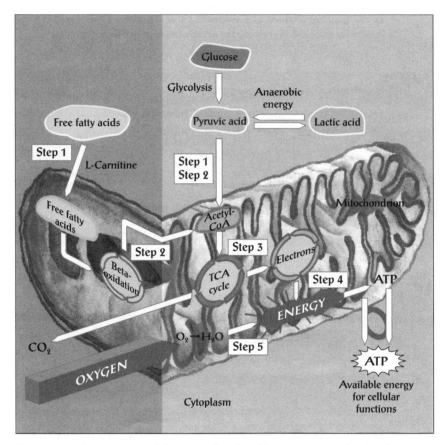

Figure 5.3 A summary of the steps involved in energy production in eukaryotes

Fat is the fuel that allows animals to travel great distances, to hunt, work, and play. This is because fat gives more energy per molecule, therefore more ATP per molecule, than does sugar. It is biochemically self-evident that since we have mitochondria, we need to eat fat.

In the primitive anaerobic organisms that inhabited the earth billions of years ago (and still exist today), only two ATP are generated from every onc molecule of glucose. Since there are six carbon atoms in glucose, this amounts to only one-third of an ATP generated per carbon atom.

Theoretically, this same glucose molecule will yield a total of thirty-six ATP molecules from mitochondrial respiration in the presence of oxygen. That's a very large increase in energy obtained from the same molecule by two different biochemical processes, and it amounts to six ATP molecules for each carbon of glucose.

Still, the energy obtained from fat is even greater. A fatty acid molecule with six carbon atoms would yield forty-eight ATP molecules from aerobic respiration inside the mitochondria. This amounts to eight ATP molecules for each carbon on a fat molecule. What we realize is that fat supplies more energy for the same amount of food, as compared to carbohydrates.

Think of it this way. Animals that are consumed by people have already used their own energy to make fat molecules, so people can get more benefit from eating animals. Even though carbohydrates from plants have some stored energy, it is less than animal fat. Why not eat more fat, fewer carbohydrates, and make your mitochondria function to full capacity as they were designed to do?

ENERGY CONSIDERATIONS IN DIFFERENT ORGANS

The Brain

Your brain uses between 150 and 200 grams of energy daily, mainly from glucose. Since we promote no more than 72 grams of utilizable carbohydrates per day, your body will need to make up the difference.

Fortunately, the body has many ways to do this. The first is a process called *gluconeogenesis*. This means "the new formation of glucose." The body can make glucose from amino acids obtained from proteins, or it can start with pyruvate. The signals to begin gluconeogenesis are sent out when glucose levels in the diet drop to low enough levels and the supply of glycogen in the liver is used up. Gluconeogenesis functions to bridge the gap until energy can be obtained from stored fat. With today's high-carbohydrate food intake, fat usage for energy is diminished. After reducing carbohydrates, it can take some time for the body to switch over to primarily using fat for energy.

By reducing carbohydrate intake, the synthesis of glucose from protein is increased. The making of glucose is an anabolic process and requires energy to build up the glucose molecule from smaller pieces. We have already shown that, with adequate fat consumption, large amounts of ATP will be generated in the mitochondria. This ATP can be used for gluconeogenesis.

This new pool of glucose can now be used for energy by the brain and other tissues. The beauty of this is that the glucose is made on an as-needed basis. This eliminates the excessive buildup of insulin and blood glucose levels that accompany excess carbohydrate consumption. And, as we pointed out in chapters 3 and 4, excessive levels of insulin over a prolonged period of time can have dire consequences.

Many of our detractors have argued that the problem with this philosophy is that the body will use up too much protein, and muscle will wither away. This assertion is based on what is known about starvation. No one can argue against the fact that in times of starvation, the body will weaken and begin to wither away. But we're not talking about starvation. We're talking about a situation where there is plenty of protein available. After seeing the results of the low-carbohydrate diet on fat and muscle growth in thousands of people, we can confidently assure our critics that no one has ever withered away. On the contrary, in the long run, people either lose fat or gain muscle—even very thin people.

Let's look at it another way. Would you rather have big muscles to supply protein for gluconeogenesis, or have big fat deposits from carbohydrates and use the stored fat for energy? Even if you choose the fat-deposit scenario, you'll have to reduce your carbohydrates in order to activate the glucagon and epinephrine hormones to burn the fat. There's just no avoiding low-carbohydrate nutrition if you want to obtain optimal health!

Another important, and often misunderstood, energy source in our cells are compounds called *ketones*. Ketones are generated from the breakdown of fatty acids in the mitochondria of liver cells and the addition of two acetyl-CoA molecules. These ketone "bodies," as they are sometimes called, are transported to various tissues through the bloodstream and converted back into acetyl-CoA to generate ATP again.

The presence of ketones in the blood and urine, a condition known as *ketosis*, has always been regarded as a negative situation, related to starvation. While it is true that ketones are generated during starvation conditions, they also are generated in times of plenty—but *not* plenty of carbohydrates. Since carbohydrate consumption suppresses fat metabolism, ketones do not form. But in the absence of most carbohydrates in the diet, ketones will form from fat to supply energy. This is true even if large amounts of protein and fat are consumed in the diet, which is hardly a starvation condition.

Your brain, as well as other tissues, can use ketone bodies for energy. So here again we see that glucose is not necessary for energy, even for the brain. But Dr. Lutz has found that the benefits of low-carbohydrate nutrition only require 72 grams or so of carbohydrate per day. This amount is not usually low enough to require the body to make ketones for energy. Nonetheless, except in certain cases of people with metabolic diseases, ketosis is not something to fear.

Remember that what is considered a "normal diet" today is based on a limited amount of data, all of which was acquired after humans already had begun eating too much carbohydrate. If you could take a trip back to the days before modern humans emerged, you might very well find that ketosis was more the normal metabolic state, and that today's human metabolic state is mostly abnormal.

The Heart and the Skeletal Tissue

It seems that no one really discusses energy in terms of organs other than the brain, which is always quoted as needing glucose. We never hear anything about the needs of the heart and other organs. One of the body's best-kept secrets is that the heart uses fatty acids almost exclusively for energy, and these are saturated fat.[1,2] This is a truly important point, and we think you can see why. How can people say that most healthy foods for the heart are low in fat, when the heart muscle is known to require fat in order to beat?

One reason could be that fatty acids can also be made from acetyl-CoA. Using this mechanism, the acetyl-CoA derived from glycolysis can make fatty acids as needed. However, it is known that fatty acid synthesis does not significantly contribute to the energy needs of the heart muscle cells.

The fact is, your heart needs fat from your diet to keep working. Low-fat diets that are also high in carbohydrate intake are probably the worst thing you could do for your heart, yet this is the prevailing theory, promoted by numerous, often misinformed, organizations and people.

The single reason that the low-fat diet is so greatly promoted is this: fear of cholesterol. Yet this is but another widespread myth that's not really consistent with available information. The next chapter on heart disease will reveal just how weak the cholesterol theory is.

CHAPTER SIX

Heart Disease: From Fat to Fiction

HEART DISEASE IS THE PRIMARY cause of death in civilized countries today. There has been a major focus on heart disease in the United States, and everyone is now familiar with the orthodox view that fat and cholesterol are the primary dietary causes of heart disease.

There are many different classifications of heart disease. *Arteriosclerosis* is the term given to hardening and calcification of the arteries. *Atherosclerosis* is the name for artery occlusions resulting from fatty deposits and cholesterol. These two types of blood flow problems are responsible for most heart disease.

For many years, the main health focus was on atherosclerosis, even though arteriosclerosis represents a significant health problem. Why might this be? We feel the reason is because only in atherosclerosis is there an association with fat and cholesterol, and there is a desire for many people to keep cholesterol as the villain in heart disease. Allegedly unbiased information is often presented in a lopsided fashion.

Stroke is another condition that is related to blood flow. Stroke is usually the term given to a condition where the blood flow to the brain has been cut off or diminished for a few minutes. Stroke usually results in paralysis of one side of the body. It typically arises from a blood clot that enters the bloodstream and then lodges in the wrong place, often due to an artery that is obstructed by a plaque or a slightly ruptured artery.

HOW IT ALL BEGAN

Before the 1950s, fat was not considered a harmful food substance. At that time, most food was considered healthy, and little attention was given to nutrition and its relation to disease. Sugar was generally regarded as harmful in excess. So why did this all change?

As the knowledge of medicine and basic science began to grow, new tools became available for understanding the biochemistry of life. Along with these advancements came a new awareness that environmental factors, such as smoking and diet, played a role in human health. Medicine generally lagged behind basic research when it came to understanding physiology and biochemistry, but made great strides in many important health-related areas.

Nutrition, however, was not one of them. Most medical schools traditionally have devoted little time to nutrition; even today there exists a mind-set that finds fat the dietary culprit, without any real exploration of the alternatives. The alternatives were to look at protein and carbohydrate as potential foods that contribute to heart disease.

Then came a few flawed studies, heralded as the beginning of a nutritional breakthrough that promised dramatic reductions in heart disease. To make matters worse, the interpretations made of the data in these flawed studies were extended to include other diseases as well. Perhaps even economic factors played a part, such as the amount of money being made in drug therapy and in the food industry that relies on maintaining the myth that fat and cholesterol cause, or increase the risk, of heart disease.

One of the great mysteries of the past fifty years is what exactly happened back in the 1950s to bring about the current conventional view that fat is harmful to peoples' health.

In order to try to solve this enigma, it is essential to revisit the studies that sparked a theory that today dominates the world view on heart health. Today, at the start of a new century, is an especially good time to do so, as rapid advancements in science and medicine have introduced more accurate methods of reevaluating older ideas. This reevaluation is an integral part of what is known as the scientific method, and is a fundamental process in science.

The scientific method takes into account new information, evaluates that information for accuracy and proper methodology, and then unites the total sum of information into a theory that best fits it all. Furthermore, all accepted theories must be open to change. Use of the scientific method has been taking place for thousands of years. If this was not the case, we would still think the Earth is flat, or that the Earth is the center of the universe.

It is vital for the useful application of the scientific method that observations be unbiased. Naturally, this is virtually impossible for humans, who have so much external input on a daily basis; yet the most objective science that can be achieved is necessary to remove the prejudices that can create inaccuracies in theories.

The difficulty with any human endeavor that involves collective thought is the summing-up of all the pieces by many people.

At some point in our scientific careers, we both decided to reevaluate as much scientific and medical information as we could, starting with eliminating any bias that was present from the broad consensus that always dominates our lives. After all, both of us used to accept the theory that fat was bad for us, and that, for some unexplained reason, carbohydrates were naturally healthy. This method of "starting from scratch" allows each individual to see more than can be seen in a group, when each only sees one piece of the information.

The famous French philosopher and mathematician René Descartes wrote a brilliant treatise on this exact method in 1637, called *Discourse on the Method of Rightly Conducting One's Reason and of Seeking Truth in the Sciences*,[1] in which he elegantly outlines a method that one can use to arrive at scientific truth, at least to the best of one's ability.

CHOLESTEROL

Cholesterol, such an important molecule in the body, has been given a bad rap. Some of you may not even realize that cholesterol is essential for life. It is the most prominent member of the steroid family of fats and an essential component of eukaryotic membranes.

Membranes are critical components of cells, separating individual organelles and the cell itself from surrounding fluids and other cells. Membrane integrity is crucial to the body's optimum function: Any breakdown in the semipermeability of membranes can result in the malfunction of cells, tissues, and even organs.

Cholesterol also is the precursor molecule to many steroid hormones, which regulate a great number of physiological functions. In addition, cholesterol can be converted to bile acids in the liver. This is one of the major pathways for cholesterol catabolism. Bile, of which cholesterol is only one component, aids in the emulsification (use) of fats for digestion, increases peristalsis (movement of the intestines), and slows the decay of fecal matter. So don't think of cholesterol as a bad molecule, but instead, remember it as one that promotes health in many ways. As you will see, the evidence against cholesterol as a factor in heart disease risk is not good evidence after all.

CLASSIFICATION OF SCIENTIFIC STUDIES

Researchers use many different types of studies to evaluate a particular question. These studies include epidemiological (population), animal, *in vivo*, and human clinical trials. All of these offer insight into the questions being explored, but each also can suffer from certain drawbacks.

Epidemiological studies were originally intended to give researchers clues about what to focus on in controlled studies. They are most useful when a transmittable disease outbreak occurs: By following disease outbreaks based on populations, epidemiologists can help to stop the spread of infectious disease.

Today, much of what is promoted regarding health and nutrition is the result of using epidemiological studies as direct *proof* for a specific health effect. Diseases that are not transmitted by a virus or bacterium are routinely evaluated by epidemiology. In the proper context, this is not necessarily a bad thing. But when the results of these types of studies are considered direct proof, then this is science gone awry.

Consider this: How can population groups be evaluated for some effect on people's health when there are so many variables in our lives? Epidemiologists use many mathematical tools to eliminate variables so that a specific variable can be studied. But in the end, all that can really be determined is a possible trend. But trends are not direct proof. The truth is, when controlled studies are conducted based on epidemiological evidence, it's very common to find that the results of the two studies do not agree.

Animal studies in a laboratory setting are much more controllable, and they, too, give insight into human diseases, but there also can be problems in relating these experiments to humans. When a drug or nutritional component is tested in humans, although it was very beneficial in animal studies, it is often found that the human response is not similar to the animal response. This is even more prevalent when animals that have very different metabolisms than humans are used to predict human relevancy.

Rabbits are a good example. Rabbits are vegetarians, yet we have based the heart disease theory in part upon the fact that rabbits get atherosclerosis when fed very large amounts of cholesterol. Humans have a feedback mechanism that stops the body from making cholesterol when it is consumed in the diet. Rabbits do not have this mechanism. It is no wonder the poor bunnies get clogged arteries when fed inordinately large amounts of cholesterol in their diets. Naturally, this would have adverse effects upon their health—their bodies were not created with the ability to deal with large amounts of dietary cholesterol.

Studies employing *in vivo* techniques in the laboratory also offer much information that is useful, but extending these types of studies to the human being is hardly ever successful. *In vivo* studies are done using bacteria, yeast, and human cell lines. Human cell lines are cells that have been removed from humans and then placed into an incubator with nutrients provided to make them grow independently. They no longer represent part of our whole organism. Thus, it's difficult to extrapolate experiments in cell line cultures back to the whole body's function.

Human studies are really the ultimate test that we have today to explore health and disease issues. This makes sense because the studies are done directly with humans. But even here science must be cautious. One of the difficulties in human clinical studies is related to time. Most diseases in humans arise as we age—the so-called "age-related diseases," such as heart disease, cancer, Type 2 diabetes, and Alzheimer's disease. In order to truly determine nutritional variables that affect these diseases, we would need to have clinical trials that lasted ten to twenty years or longer. This is not practical, particularly in prevention studies.

Our natural longevity on the evolutionary scale is also a problem when it comes to determining environmental factors related to disease. Much of the dietary data available today are the result of very short studies. The information in this book from Dr. Lutz's practice is based on patients who were studied for up to three years or more to determine the long-term trends associated with a reduction in carbohydrates on their diseases.

In the next few sections, we will present some of the most popular studies that have been used to prove the fat theory. Each one is a major epidemiological study that marked the beginning of the paradigm shift away from fat as a healthy food.

THE SEVEN COUNTRIES STUDY

The Seven Countries study was the first huge undertaking of its kind. Originally, it was intended to find correlations in the types of foods consumed (and other lifestyle factors) with death rates and various diseases within different population groups in the world. Although the main emphasis was cardiovascular health, other diseases, including cancer and stroke, and overall mortality (total deaths from all causes) were also followed. At the time, this was a reasonable study to undertake since it had already been shown that there are differences in cardiovascular heart disease (CHD) among different population groups. Upon close observation, however, the Seven Countries study has many flaws; taken together, these defects make the study's conclusions very difficult to accept.

The Seven Countries study, *Seven Countries: A Multivariate Analysis of Death and Coronary Heart Disease,*[2] was published as a book in 1980. In 1994, a follow-up book, *Lessons for Science from the Seven Countries Study,*[3] was published.

According to the introductory page in the first book, the Seven Countries study was aimed at finding "individual characteristics in apparently healthy middle-aged men related to future tendency to develop cardiovascular heart disease (CHD)." The seven countries were the United States, Yugoslavia (Croatia), Japan, Italy, the Netherlands, Finland, and Greece. There were a total of sixteen different groups distributed within these countries comprising 12,763 men. The data in the first book summarized the years between the late 1940s and late 1950s as a ten-year evaluation of CHD incidence and death rates. In a rather complicated presentation of many numbers and graphs, the study is intended to support the overall conclusions—namely, that many of the risk factors reviewed do correlate with CHD. However, one of the fundamental flaws in this effort was already in place even before the work began.

At the beginning, the researchers decided which risk factors to follow. This in itself is not necessarily bad since many constraints exist that make practical choices necessary. The risk factors chosen included blood pressure, physical activity, and smoking habits. Cholesterol level and diet were picked, as well. And here is where the problems begin: Even though there are three basic components of food (protein, fat, carbohydrate), the researchers chose only to look at dietary fat intake. Apparently, they had already decided that fat was bad—very poor science, indeed.

Certainly, all three components should have been judged as potentially important in CHD and death rates. Indeed, as we shall see later from the 1994 follow-up book, when protein and carbohydrate consumption were taken into account, decreases in some diseases correlated with higher fat and lower carbohydrate intake!

One of the graphs in the book presents the all-cause, age-related, ten-year death rates of the sixteen groups versus serum cholesterol levels. Cholesterol content of the blood had absolutely *no correlation* with all-cause death rates. Even more interesting is that death rates were *lower* in many groups that had *higher* cholesterol levels!

This is an important point: Namely, that actual total death rates for all reasons, not just heart disease, had *no* correlation with cholesterol in this study. Correlation means that if a graph is made between two sets of data, a straight line can be drawn between the data points. The straighter the line, the greater the correlation. The straightness is determined mathematically and is called a "correlation coefficient." The closer the correlation coefficient is to the number one, the better the correlation.

The correlation coefficient for the data that compare the all-cause death rates with cholesterol is given in the book as 0.12. The conclusion that the authors make from these data is ". . . 0.12 is a value too small to be considered significant. This does not mean that serum cholesterol is therefore unimportant as a risk factor for all-cause death; the conclusion is only that the differences in the all-causes death rates among these groups (of people) cannot be explained by the cholesterol levels."

This type of language is pervasive throughout the book, where the authors make every attempt to dissuade the reader, and themselves, when the data do not match their initial precepts! It's almost as if they *had* to show cholesterol was bad. The reality is, if the all-cause death rates cannot be explained by the cholesterol levels, then cholesterol probably is not a risk factor for all-cause death. Pretty simple, wouldn't you say?

Now, the data relating total calories from fat in the diet to death rates from the first Seven Countries study gives a correlation coefficient of 0.50. This is not a particularly good number, either. From the data in the graph (not shown here), it is clearly seen that some countries with a higher fat intake—up to 40 percent of total calories or more—have lower death rates. In this case, the death rates are from heart disease only. Other countries have low fat intake, yet death rates are high. Still other countries have high fat intake and higher death rates from heart disease. Given an unbiased point-of-view, these data could have been interpreted two different ways: Either fat actually is suppressing heart disease or it's contributing to heart disease. The conclusions should have been that there are no conclusions!

Even more interesting is that the authors state, in one paragraph in the middle of the book, that *sugar intake was correlated with heart disease.* They offer no data for this, even though the book is more than 200 pages long. Nothing else is ever said on the subject, and no other reference is ever made to this amazing statement. Neither is there any discussion of carbohydrate intake, and there is only a little talk about dietary protein.

Since we have only three major macronutrients in our food, why did they focus only on fat? We'll never know the reason for this, but surely we cannot trust information that is so narrowly focused.

The information presented in the second book is a follow up study in which the same population groups were analyzed for different diseases for thirty-five years. Since Japan is known to have lower heart disease rates than the United States, the recent study results are noteworthy.

In the introduction section for the Japan results, the authors state that in 1958, at the beginning of the Seven Countries study, the Japanese groups had the lowest saturated fat intake and lowest blood levels of cholesterol, and were among the lowest incidence of coronary heart disease. Notice that they used the words "among the lowest." The authors carefully chose their words because, as we have said, low levels of heart disease were also observed in countries with much higher fat intake.

The trends in Japan from 1958 to 1989 showed that carbohydrate consumption decreased from 78 percent of total calories to 61 percent. Fat consumption increased from 5 percent to 22 percent. Protein consumption increased from 11 percent to 16 percent. Most of these changes were attributed to more meat, fish, and dairy products, and less rice.

In this same time period, deaths from stroke declined from 4.6 per 1,000 people to 0.8 per 1,000 people. Cancer rates also dropped slightly, from 4.7 per 1,000 people to 3.4 per 1,000 people.

Myocardial infarction remained about the same. Since smoking declined in the same period, it is likely that this played a role in the reduction of cancer and stroke. However these data are interpreted, increases in fat and protein have not proven detrimental, and have perhaps even benefited the Japanese populations that were studied.

The last paragraph in the Japanese section from the 1994 follow-up Seven Countries study states, "We conclude that the changed composition of the Japanese diet has probably improved health and reduced stroke rates. However, careful surveillance is needed in the future because of the increasing intake of fats, especially saturated fatty acids, with the potential of a modern epidemic of coronary disease in Japan."

This is a classic example of denial! Why didn't the researchers speculate that lower carbohydrate and higher fat and protein might in fact be beneficial since they observed this in their own study? Conclusions like these from respected researchers are why so many millions have succumbed to the fat theory. Once a person publicly states personal views, they will rarely change them. It is ironic that the title of the follow-up book is called *Lessons for Science*, since it is obvious that parts of science have not learned a lesson at all.

When the original Seven Countries data were published, many people took note. This is what spawned the new age of research into fat and cholesterol, particularly in the United States. When the second book was published, nobody paid attention. But even follow-up studies in the United States were unable to provide proof of the fat theory, as we shall show you next.

THE FIELD STUDIES

Following the new information from the original Seven Countries study, scientists in the United States, England, and Scandinavia initiated many field studies that were supposed to prove that animal fats and cholesterol in our diet really did cause a higher incidence of heart disease—that they are the villains that would make us sick and eventually kill us. Such attempts at proof were never really successful. Yet over the years, researchers designed more new studies under different conditions because they simply could not believe that they weren't able to prove the correctness of the fat theory! This is not the way science is supposed to work: Theories are never proved— they are just *disproved.*

But it very often appears to be the case that when someone sets out to prove something in which they have a vested interest, it will get proven somehow, some way. Results of some studies even showed that people who eat more fat live longer[4,5]—impossible! Researchers now had to resort to even bigger and better-designed studies.

One such study was the Framingham Heart Study. This was started in 1948 and involved about 6,000 men. In this study, researchers found that those who consumed more saturated fat and cholesterol in their diet actually weighed less and had a lower risk for heart disease. Yet this study is often cited by many people to *prove* that fat is harmful. One doctor who was the associate director of the study for three years, George Mann, determined that the study indicated fat is healthy, and low fat is unhealthy. He has edited a book called *Coronary Heart Disease: The Dietary Sense and Nonsense* that provides powerful evidence that saturated fat is not the cause of heart disease.[6] Mann also published observations about the good health of the Masai warriors of Kenya, Africa. His paper, "Diet Heart, End of an Era"[7] describes that, despite the intake of large amounts of fat from meat and milk, the Masai were heart disease–free.

The largest of the early studies was the MRFIT (Multiple Risk Factor Intervention Trial).[8] It included more than 12,000 male Americans who were thought to be at increased coronary risk (due to hypertension, high cholesterol level, and/or smoking). The subjects were randomly assigned to one of two groups. Randomization assured that the more than 6,000 subjects in each group were comparable with respect to risk factors, so that one could expect an equal number of heart attacks and other coronary symptoms in each group.

In the intervention group, patients were instructed to quit smoking, to avoid animal fats in favor of fats with polyunsaturated fatty acids, and to avoid dietary cholesterol as much as possible. Furthermore, they received drug treatment for their hypertension. The patients in the control group were referred to their physician without receiving any instructions at all.

Although the patients in the intervention group complied, that is, smoked less and ate fewer animal fats and cholesterol, the results were disappointing. So, an even stricter restriction of fats and cholesterol was recommended. Six years later, the final results of the study were not any more satisfying to the investigators. There was a slight reduction in deaths due to heart attacks, but the overall mortality rate was higher in the intervention group compared to the control group, due to cancer.[9]

The investigators had all kinds of excuses for these results. The medical public, however, particularly in the United States, was very disillusioned and not willing to spend a lot of money on more such studies.

In our opinion, the problem with the study design was the attempt to manipulate more than one factor at a time: smoking, cholesterol, animal fats, and hypertension. There is no doubt that smoking is detrimental to health. It has been known for decades that the arteriosclerotic process in the leg ("smoker's leg") can be accelerated with nicotine. Furthermore, a gigantic study by the American Cancer Society, observing more than a million Americans for twenty years, showed that individuals who smoke more than twenty cigarettes per day die on the average 8.3 years earlier than nonsmokers.[10]

Since the MRFIT actually succeeded in markedly reducing cigarette consumption in the intervention group, these subjects should have done much better than they actually did. Therefore, one could ask whether the low-cholesterol and low-fat diet of the intervention group possibly was harmful and actually compensated for the beneficial effect of reduced smoking.

Another interpretation of the MRFIT study showed that smokers did not have more cancers than nonsmokers. According to the American Cancer Society study mentioned earlier, cigarette smoking not only causes lung cancer but also cancer at other sites. This points in the same direction: Since smokers should have had many more cancers than nonsmokers, it follows that the subjects in the control group who did not reduce their cigarette consumption at all or not as much as the intervention group were, to some extent, protected against the consequences of smoking by more cholesterol and animal fats in their diet. This is an almost apocalyptic idea, but there are hardly any arguments against it, since a high cholesterol level seems to protect the body against anemia, infections, and cancer.

At the end of 1983, the results of another large American field study were released, called the Lipid Research Clinics Coronary Primary Prevention Trial (LRCCPPT).[11] This trial also compared two groups of patients with increased coronary risk, and followed them an average of 7.4 years. Both groups received a moderate cholesterol-reducing diet (reduction of animal fats and their substitution by highly unsaturated fats) that did not prove very effective. Next, one group additionally received the exchange resin colestyramine, which binds bile acids in the gut and thereby reduces the blood cholesterol levels. This group showed a reduction in coronary deaths of 24 percent and a reduction in survived heart attacks of 19 percent compared to controls. But here also, the overall mortality was similar in both groups: More deaths of other causes occurred in the treatment group. This study considered only a special group of patients with disorders of the fat metabolism, so that the results could not be universally applicable to begin with.

Previous field studies had come to the same conclusion—by lowering the blood cholesterol level, the coronary risk can be slightly reduced—even if the studies were not executed with such meticulous precision as the MRFIT and LRCCPPT studies. At best, a slight decrease in heart disease was shown to be associated with reduced intake of animal fat and cholesterol.

These early studies certainly do not represent a home run when it comes to determining the cause of heart disease. Since overall mortality rates varied little or increased, in all these studies, this should have been a warning sign. After all, the only real difference in whether one dies of a heart attack or of cancer is that the former goes fast and the latter goes slow. In the end, there still is mortality.

In addition, Professor R. E. Olson, who was appointed by the American Research Agency to review the literature for a harmful effect of cholesterol-containing foods, came to the conclusion that the evidence was insufficient to recommend a general restriction of animal fats and cholesterol.[12] And many other scientists agreed, among them the Swiss professor Hans Mohler, who arrived at the same conclusion in his book *Cholesterol Neurosis.*[13]

All of these studies are the basis for the low-fat fad that has dominated the world for the last thirty or more years, yet they all failed to actually prove that fat is harmful.

RECENT EPIDEMIOLOGICAL STUDIES

New information from long-term, large study groups is now becoming available. The two studies discussed in this section represent the best attempt to date at using epidemiology as a tool to interpret dietary factors and their relationship to disease. In the Nurses Health Study, more than 80,000 nurses between the ages of thirty-four and fifty-nine were followed from 1980 to 1994. In the Health Professionals Follow-up Study, more than 37,000 men between the ages of forty and seventy-five were followed from 1984 to 1994.

Researchers at Harvard University spearheaded both of these studies. In evaluating the data they now have at their disposal, the Harvard researchers asked numerous questions that have often been overlooked in previous studies. One of these concerns the consumption of eggs. Egg consumption has been villainized for years in the United States without any significant research to prove damage to health. Since it was thought that cholesterol was bad for the body, eggs—which are high in cholesterol—also were assumed to be detrimental to health.

A recently published article from both of the studies cited above[14] evaluated the information from the large study groups to determine any association between egg consumption and the risk of cardiovascular heart disease and stroke. The dietary patterns of 37,851 men and 80,082 women were evaluated. The authors found no evidence of egg consumption as a contributor to heart disease. In both men and women, five to six eggs per week slightly reduced the incidence of heart disease events, but slightly elevated risks were observed for men who ate an average of one to three or more than six per week. For women, there was no increase in the risk of cardiovascular disease for any amount of eggs consumed per week. The authors concluded that eating "up to one egg per day" is unlikely to contribute to heart disease in healthy men and women. One wonders what the results would be for people who eat two to three eggs per day; this information was not presented. Very few people in this study probably ate that many eggs each day, anyway.

In another set of published studies from the Nurses Health Study, researchers found that frequent nut consumption was associated with a decreased risk of both fatal coronary heart disease and nonfatal myocardial infarction.[15] Nuts contain mostly fat and protein, which is consistent with a low-carbohydrate diet. A typical ratio of fat, protein, and carbohydrate for mixed nuts is 18 grams of fat, 5 grams of protein, and 7 grams of carbohydrate in a 33-gram serving.

In still another published paper from the Nurses Health Study, epidemiologists found that increased intake of protein resulted in a decreased risk for ischemic heart disease.[16] The authors concluded that, in contrast to the hypothesis that dietary protein increases the risk of heart disease, replacing carbohydrates with protein may be associated with a lower risk of ischemic heart disease. The authors are cautious though, and they add that since increased protein is associated with higher animal fat and cholesterol consumption, the public should be cautious. Perhaps it is the saturated animal fat that accompanies the higher protein intake that lowers the risk!

It seems clear from these studies that the new evidence from the larger groups of people suggests the role of carbohydrate as the dietary component that contributes to heart disease. Certainly, increased fat and protein consumption are not resulting in any increase in heart disease. Along with higher fat and greater protein intake comes a natural reduction in carbohydrates, because fat and protein-containing foods have little carbohydrate content.

On May 5, 1999, Dr. Walter Willett spoke at a seminar at the National Institutes of Health (NIH) in Bethesda, Maryland. Dr. Willett is chairman of the Department of Nutrition and Professor of Medicine at Harvard University, and his talk was entitled, "Diet and Heart Disease: Have We Misled the Nation?" Willett is the principal author of all the cited studies from the Nurses Health Study and the Health Professionals Follow-up Study.

In his NIH presentation, Willett pointed out that the Seven Countries data are not supportive of the "fat is bad for us" theory. We discussed this study earlier in the chapter. He also presented other data indicating that the glycemic index of foods has some association to heart disease—that is, the higher the glycemic index, the greater the risk of heart disease. The glycemic index is a measure of how much glucose, and therefore insulin, is produced after ingesting the food. Simply put, it is a reasonable measure of how much utilizable carbohydrate is in the food. We look forward to the publication of the data Willett mentioned that specifically follows carbohydrate consumption and its relation to disease.

HOMOCYSTEINE

One of the most important discoveries in medical research this century is the theory of homocysteine and its relationship to not only heart disease but also cancer and other age-related diseases. Homocysteine is an amino acid that contains sulfur. Amino acids are the molecules that comprise proteins. Proteins are larger biomolecules that contain many amino acids linked together by chemical bonds. Homocysteine is not used directly in proteins; rather, it is an intermediate substance that can be converted into the amino acids methionine or cystcine, both of which are used directly in proteins.

In 1933, a pathologist at Massachusetts General Hospital noted clinical features in an eight-year-old boy that suggested the child had died from arteriosclerosis—a most unusual situation. After many years of medical detective work, Dr. Kilmer McCully, an American researcher and pathologist, was able to put together the pieces of this intriguing puzzle.

What McCully discovered was that excess homocysteine in the blood can lead to heart disease. Twenty years ago, when he was trying to inform the medical and scientific communities of the problem, this idea was considered quite controversial. At that time, cholesterol was considered the hot item in heart disease research, and McCully was going against the establishment, much as Dr. Lutz did with his low-carbohydrate research. McCully paid dearly for his beliefs—many colleagues abandoned him, and Harvard refused to renew his research grants. Yet today, the homocysteine theory of disease is recognized as an important factor in arteriosclerosis.

The theory of homocysteine and its relationships to heart disease is simple. Excess homocysteine in the blood can cause chemical reactions that tend to make low-density lipoproteins (LDL) adhere to arterial tissue. In chemical terms, this means that homocysteine can cause LDL to build up in arteries. Low-density lipoproteins are proteins that transport lipids to various parts of the body. They are an important and necessary component of the body's protein and fat pool; for instance, cholesterol is transported to various tissues and cells by these proteins. LDL is considered bad cholesterol, but it really is not just cholesterol. It is a protein that has many cholesterol molecules attached to it.

The homocysteine theory is based on sound scientific and medical experimentation. McCully has published more than eighty scientific and medical articles on his discoveries and about building the homocysteine theory of arteriosclerosis. He has also published two books outlining his conclusions and how they affect each of us,[17,18] and what he has found is that deficiencies of three vitamins can lead to excess levels of homocysteine. This medical condition is called *hyperhomocysteinemia*.

The three vitamins are B_6, B_{12}, and folic acid. These vitamins are components of three different proteins that are used to metabolize homocysteine. A deficiency, or metabolic imbalance that appears as a deficiency, of any of these can lead to excess homocysteine in the blood because our cells cannot metabolize the homocysteine. Elevated levels of homocysteine result from this, and high levels potentially allow the homocysteine to damage tissue by detrimental chemical reactions.

So how does this fit in with reduced carbohydrates in the diet? That's easy: All three vitamins are found in animal foods. Vitamin B_{12} is only found in animal foods. Vitamins B_6 and folic acid are found in fish, poultry, other meats, and green leafy vegetables—that is, in low-carbohydrate foods. Diets high in carbohydrates, particularly processed, refined carbohydrates, offer little in the way of these vitamins. In 1998, this idea was confirmed. A study published in the *Netherland Journal of Medicine* has revealed that vegetarians and vegans have higher levels of homocysteine compared to people who have high fat and meat intakes![19]

It became clear, in numerous discussions with Kilmer McCully, that he offers extremely powerful evidence to displace the fat theory of heart disease. As a pathologist, he has looked directly at damaged arterial tissue. What he finds, over and over again, is that most patients who die of severe heart disease have relatively normal cholesterol levels.

In one research study published in 1990,[20] McCully evaluated by autopsy the severity of heart disease in 194 people. He then compared cholesterol levels from their previous medical records to their severity of heart disease. What he found should shock you.

The average cholesterol level in people with the most severe heart disease was 186 mg/dl. Generally, 186 mg/dl is considered normal or even low for heart disease relationships. Although there was a large spread in the numbers, this goes against everything the public has been led to believe.

However, studies like this one are rare. Even though there have been unprecedented amounts of research done on cholesterol and heart disease in recent years, no one ever bothered to do direct comparisons between the two until McCully published this work ten years ago. Certainly it is true that cholesterol deposits are sometimes found inside arteries of people who have died of heart disease—the problem is that elevated cholesterol levels are a poor marker for this happening. The homocysteine theory, based on exemplary chemical, biochemical, and medical data, leaves no doubt that this primary substance has a greater association with heart disease than cholesterol alone. There will certainly be more information about homocysteine as this theory gets scrutinized, but just the fact that cholesterol levels have a poor correlation with heart disease is sufficient to require a change in the brainwashing of America.

STUDIES ON CHICKENS

Before we look at the profound beneficial effects of low-carbohydrate nutrition on various risk factors associated with human heart disease, let's examine the results obtained with chickens fed low-carbohydrate nutrition. Chickens were chosen for these studies for many reasons. An animal was needed that fulfilled numerous criteria for nutrition experiments. First, it had to be known to exhibit some type of arteriosclerosis in old age that was similar to humans. It also had to be easy to maintain and also not live too long. The animal had to be an omnivore in the wild. The domestic fowl was the animal that fit this description. In this animal, arteriosclerosis becomes apparent in the third or fourth year of life. Just as in humans, arteriosclerosis begins in the abdominal portion of the aorta and then spreads to the other parts of the vessel. Both histologically and biochemically, arteriosclerosis in chickens resembles that in humans. Chickens eat insects and other small creatures in the wild. They are not grain eaters, unless they are in captivity.

Dr. Lutz and his colleagues, who performed these studies, decided on three different amounts of carbohydrate in the diet of the experimental chickens. The chickens were fed either 18, 43, or 73 percent of the food as carbohydrate. All the chickens were of the same genetic pool. The animals were fed mostly milk, eggs, dried shrimps, pork meat, and beef bone meal, as a replacement of carbo-hydrate. Very little unsaturated fatty acids were eaten. Most of the fat was saturated fat. The carbohydrate was wheat grains. The chickens were allowed to eat freely, and the amount of food avail-able was in excess of what was required for simple survival.

The results of these animal studies showed that the worst cases of arteriosclerosis in chickens were in those that ate the largest percent-age of their food as carbohydrates.[21] Two different measurements were made in this determination. First, the larger arteries were visually in-spected and given a rating as to the extent of arteriosclerosis. These evaluations were performed by a third party, Andresen, at that time an assistant professor at Weitzel's Institute of Biochemistry, Tübingen, Germany. Second, the total amount of fat associated with the aorta was chemically measured after it was removed from the chickens since the amount of fat associated with the aorta should be partially repre-sentative of the degree of atherosclerosis. Both the total amount of fat associated with the aorta and the occurrence of arteriosclerosis (macroscopic evaluation) was greater in the animals fed the most car-bohydrates. These results are summarized in Table 6.1. These exper-iments were repeated, and the results were confirmed.[22]

A lot of other observations were made on these animals that can be of use in understanding our human diseases. The total calories consumed by the animals increased as the amount of carbohydrate increased. The general argument that it is only calories that deter-mine nutritional related diseases is not altogether true. Clearly, based on the fact that chickens ate more calories when more carbo-hydrates were supplied, this suggests that there is either an addictive effect from carbohydrates, or that the body is not getting what it needs, and so the signal to eat more is present.

The chickens fed the lowest amounts of carbohydrate produced the fewest eggs. This indicates that carbohydrates do have a direct effect on hormones, as we have already shown in chapters 2 and 3. It is not normal for wild animals to produce as many eggs as farm chickens do. They are fed large amounts of grain and corn products,

Table 6.1 Details of the fat (lipid) analysis and occurrence of arteriosclerosis in chickens fed varying amounts of carbohydrate in their diet.

Group	Number of Animals	Percent Carbohydrate In the Diet	Total Lipids In the Aorta (% dry weight)	Macroscopic Occurrence of Arteriosclerosis
I	5	18	19.4	1.1
II	7	43	20.2	1.9
III	5	73	24.5	2.8

Source: W. Lutz, G. Andresen, and F. Buddecke. "Uber den Einfluss kohlenhydratarmer Diaten auf de Artierosklerose des Huhnes." *Zeitschr. 2. Enhrungswissensch* 9 (1969): 22.

and this is what is responsible for the high egg production. Perhaps this extends to humans as well. When large amounts of carbohydrates were introduced during the agricultural revolution some 8,000 years ago, the population began to rapidly grow. Chapter 11 on evolution explores the effects of the transition from a hunter/gatherer to a farmer in more detail.

RISK FACTORS AND CARBOHYDRATE RESTRICTION IN HUMANS

The next question is, what happens to the risk factors associated with heart disease when carbohydrates are reduced in the diet? Low-carbohydrate nutrition is associated with the consumption of larger amounts of animal fats and cholesterol. According to the fat theory, this type of diet is supposed to have atherogenic potential, that is, actually should enhance the development of atherosclerosis. Over the years, Dr. Lutz has accumulated a veritable mountain of information that indicates just the opposite.

Polycythemia

Many studies have shown that an elevated level of blood pigment, or more precisely, an increased number of blood cells per unit of volume, is associated with a considerably elevated risk of cardiac infarction from blood clots. Approximately 25 percent of all North Americans have hemoglobin levels approaching the upper limit of the norm, and these individuals do have more heart attacks than people with lower levels.

Hemoglobin is the protein that gives the red color to the blood of humans and most animals. Hemoglobin is contained within the red blood cells; it transports oxygen from the lungs to all body tissues, then takes carbon dioxide from the tissues back to the lungs for removal through exhalation.

The concentration of hemoglobin protein is 15 to 16 g/dl in healthy males and 14 to 15 g/dl in healthy females. The risk of heart attacks and strokes increases when hemoglobin rises above the lower limit of the norm, that is, when females have a level above 14 g/dl and males a level above 15 g/dl. A hemoglobin level that is too high can result in thickening of the blood, which could cause decreased blood flow if there is any obstruction in the arteries and veins.

There are individuals who have more hemoglobin than they should. This disorder is called *polycythemia*, which means that these patients have too many red blood cells. Since the hemoglobin load of each red blood cell is generally constant, the concentration of blood pigment per unit of volume increases with the number of red blood cells. For example, individuals who have six or seven million red blood cells, instead of five million, will have 19 or 22 grams of hemoglobin in one-tenth of a liter of blood, instead of the usual amount of 16 grams.

In polycythemia, then, the blood is too thick and has a strong tendency to clot, which leads to heart attacks and strokes. So it's easy to understand how a hemoglobin level above the lower limit of the norm constitutes a risk factor.

Happily, polycythemia responds perfectly to a low-carbohydrate diet. Figure 6.1 shows what happens to the hemoglobin levels in 130 people who adopted a low-carbohydrate diet. You can see that there is a rapid reduction after only fifteen days. The levels continue to decline and begin to level off after thirty months on the diet.

You might be thinking that this seems illogical since a low-carbohydrate diet means an increase in meat consumption, which itself contains hemoglobin. Instead, this finding confirms the fact that lowering the amount of carbohydrate you eat influences many aspects of your physiology by placing your body in the correct balance, so that its biochemical reactions can normalize.

This reduction of hemoglobin in individuals with high levels is typical and regular—so much so, in fact, that we suggest the common form of polycythemia (for which no particular cause is known) be renamed "carbohydrate-dependent polycythemia."

There are other forms of this disorder besides the common form already mentioned. One of these is a red blood malignancy known as *Polycythemia rubra vera*, which shows associations to the leukemias (malignancies of white blood cells). It is characterized by an enlarged spleen and increase in white blood cells and blood platelets. These cases tend to worsen under carbohydrate restriction.

In so-called symptomatic polycythemia, the number of red blood cells tends to increase. There are situations in which a higher number of red blood cells is required in order to overcome a compromised gas exchange: Inhabitants of the Andes Mountains, who live at an elevation of 3,000 to 4,000 meters and accordingly breathe thin air, have such symptomatic polycythemia. Europeans who migrate to high elevations, in time, also get this type of polycythemia. Thick blood is necessary in these high elevations to assure that, despite low oxygen pressure in the air, the body's tissues are sufficiently oxygenated. The fact that one of the most important risk factors for heart attack and stroke can be treated dietetically, via the red blood pigment hemoglobin, is of great practical significance to people around the world.

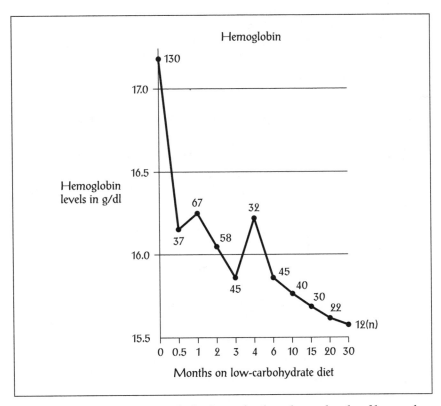

Figure 6.1 A reduction in carbohydrates leads to lower levels of hemoglobin in the blood, which is associated with a decreased risk of heart disease. Hemoglobin levels of 130 patients were initially evaluated. The numbers at each data point are the amount of people evaluated and averaged at that time.

Hypertension

Another risk factor for heart disease is high blood pressure, or hypertension. Figure 6.2 shows the blood pressure of thirty-eight patients with moderate hypertension, in response to a diet of 72 grams

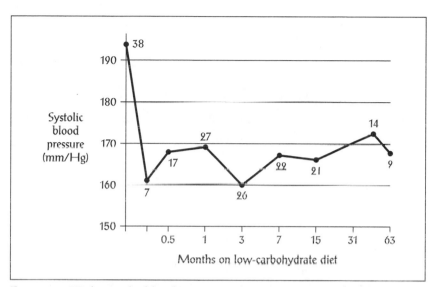

Figure 6.2 High systolic blood pressure, a known risk for heart disease, decreases when a low-carbohydrate diet is employed. Initially, thirty-eight people were evaluated. The numbers at each point are the amount of people measured at the given time. The decrease in blood pressure is maintained for over five years, which represents a stable, long-term condition.

of carbohydrate per day. Many more patients with hypertension have been observed over the years by Dr. Lutz, probably close to 500, but in this study only those who never had to take antihypertensive medication during the observation period were included, since such medication naturally would have obscured the results.

This is also the reason why the average initial blood pressure prior to the diet reached only 193 mm/Hg. Patients with higher blood pressures usually require medication and they do not respond as well to the diet; under carbohydrate restriction, though, the blood pressure rarely rises any further.

Results from the study found that the systolic blood pressure dropped immediately (in this case to an average of 161 mm/Hg) and after two weeks rose again slightly. It finally stabilized at a level 20 mm/Hg below the initial value. Certainly the fact that patients are more nervous at the time of initial pressure reading than later during control measurements may play a role. However, a drop in blood pressure with carbohydrate restriction can still be demonstrated when the initial measurement is taken several times during the first few days. This same result was observed in 1952 by a Delaware physician, who noted that high blood pressure dropped under a low-carbohydrate diet, and it was parallel to weight loss.[23]

Malignant Hypertension

Among the several thousand patients on a low-carbohydrate diet in Dr. Lutz's practice, there were some juveniles with protein excretion in the urine and blood vessel lesions on the retina, a so-called *hypertension retinopathy*. These youngsters also had symptoms that usually are summarized under the heading "malignant hypertension." Within a short time—usually only a few months—all symptoms, including the retinal lesions, had disappeared in all these cases solely due to the carbohydrate restriction.

As mentioned before, elevated blood pressure in older individuals often cannot be normalized or lowered. We would still recommend putting such people on a low-carbohydrate diet, while following the precautions recommended at the end of this book. We believe that the danger of vessel rupture and, consequently, the risk of a stroke due to brain hemorrhaging is lowered, while, at the same time, cardiac output is increased. It has been noted that patients on this diet feel strikingly well in contrast to patients treated with medication.

Once the situation has stabilized to a reasonable extent, and if the blood pressure is still too high, then antihypertensive medication can be given. Antihypertensive medications often aggravate concurrent diabetes.

Uric Acid and Kidney Stones

An elevated level of uric acid is another risk factor, the significance of which has been noted for years. The uric acid present in humans is a metabolite of dietary protein and nucleotides (or nucleic acids), both components of the cell nucleus.

High blood levels of uric acid are associated with deposition of uric acid in tissues, in urinary stones, or in the kidneys. With a low-carbohydrate diet, the intake of meat, and therefore that of nucleic acids and proteins, is increased. Consequently, the uric-acid levels should rise.

However, exactly the opposite happens. Figure 6.3 shows what happened to 193 patients with elevated uric acid levels under a low-carbohydrate diet. As you can see, the concentration of uric acid

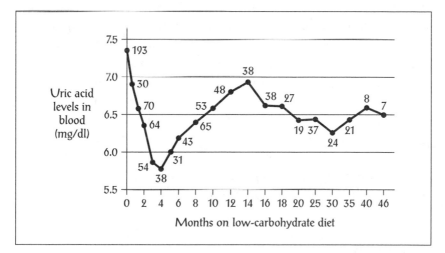

Figure 6.3 Uric acid levels in the blood of 193 patients who initially had elevated levels. The levels drop immediately when a low-carbohydrate diet is consumed. After almost four years, the blood levels stabilize well below the initial values. The numbers at any one point represent the number of patients measured at the indicated time.

dropped immediately and reached a low point after four months. From then on, it slowly increased again until it stabilized at an intermediate value. The diet has a definite lowering effect on uric acid. Therefore, one may conclude that high uric-acid levels are caused at least partially by dietary carbohydrates.

For a long time, it has been known that infusion of sugar solutions, especially fructose and sorbitol, cause a quick elevation of uric acid. This is due to an overproduction of uric acid and not due to lowered excretion, because the rise in uric acid after sugar infusion can be suppressed by the body, using allopurinol. Allopurinol inhibits the enzyme xanthine oxidase, which aids in the production of uric acid. So it seems that carbohydrates stimulate uric-acid production. This alone should be a reason to put people with elevated uric-acid levels on a carbohydrate-restricted diet.

While Figure 6.3 shows the reaction of elevated uric-acid levels to carbohydrate restriction, Figure 6.4 shows eleven patients whose uric-acid level initially dropped very suddenly but then rose again above the initial value. This explains why the graph in Figure 6.3 looks a little strange. Once the individuals who all experienced a rise in uric-acid levels are separated, then the bottom curve in Figure 6.4 shows a permanent lowering effect. The fact that some levels rose over time shows that there certainly are cases of individuals who depart from the norm and experience a further rise in uric acid after a carbohydrate-restrictive diet is in place. The patients whose uric-acid levels increased had parallel changes in their cholesterol levels. These people probably had a metabolic disorder that was uncorrectable by a low-carbohydrate diet.

CHOLESTEROL

As we have shown in this chapter, cholesterol is, at most, a small risk factor for heart disease, and certainly not the causative factor. This statement is based on the fact that most people with severe heart

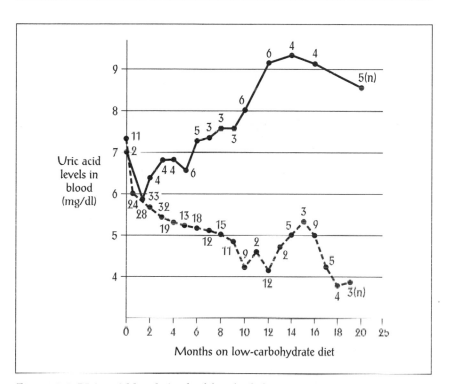

Figure 6.4 Uric acid levels in the blood of eleven patients (*upper curve*) who initially had a decrease, but whose levels became elevated at a later time. In these eleven patients, the uric acid levels rose and fell parallel to cholesterol levels, indicating that an underlying metabolic disorder existed in these people.

disease who have been tested have a somewhat normal cholesterol level. While we feel that cholesterol gets too much attention as a risk factor for heart disease, it is instructive to look at what happens to cholesterol levels when people adopt a low-carbohydrate diet.

We have heard from many people that their doctors tell them that a low-carbohydrate, high-fat diet causes a huge increase in cholesterol. Most likely these doctors do not have scientific evidence that this is true. They have probably read it in the paper, seen a few talks at a medical convention, or are being misled by pharmaceutical sales

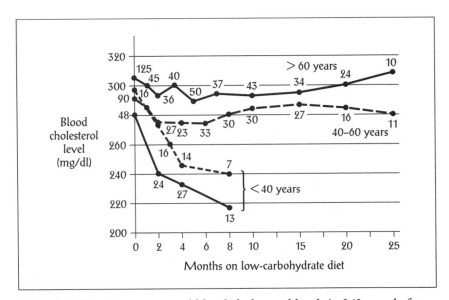

Figure 6.5 The changes in total blood cholesterol levels in 263 people for different age groups after adopting a low-carbohydrate diet. *Top curve*, age group above sixty years; *middle curve*, age group between forty and sixty years; *bottom two curves*, age group less than forty years. In the group under forty years of age, cholesterol drops immediately under carbohydrate restriction; at an older age there is no significant change. The drop in the younger age group is not due to the initial lower level because a higher initial level, *dotted line curve*, also decreases with the diet.

representatives who are pushing their cholesterol-lowering drugs. However, we have convincing proof of falling cholesterol levels in people of different ages who adopt a low-carbohydrate diet over the long term.

Figure 6.5 shows the results of blood cholesterol levels for 263 patients who were followed for up to twenty-five months. It turns out that the cholesterol level almost always dropped following implementation of a low-carbohydrate diet. And the higher the initial level and the younger the patient, the more extensive and the more stable was the effect.

This result is surprising only if you believe that high cholesterol comes from high-fat diets. The low-carbohydrate diet contains more animal fats and more cholesterol than the standard diet consumed in the United States or the diet the patients ate prior to the experiment. The cholesterol level of the diet lies approximately 50 percent above what the general population takes in, and therefore probably above what the patients ate prior to the carbohydrate restriction. Yet patients' blood cholesterol levels dropped, despite a large increase in the consumption of cholesterol and animal fats.

These results topple one of the pillars of the fat theory, namely, the idea that high dietary intake of animal fats and cholesterol is an important risk factor for arteriosclerosis. According to the fat theory, high plasma levels of triglycerides and cholesterol are the primary causes of arteriosclerosis. Yet it is well known that triglycerides arise primarily from carbohydrate in the diet. Triglycerides are the stored form of carbohydrates in adipose tissue. Dr. Lutz's patients all had a decrease of triglycerides after adopting a low-carbohydrate diet, and this has been well documented in many, many studies. The levels of triglycerides in 118 patients in Dr Lutz's practice dropped an average of more than 50 percent after only three months on a low-carbohydrate diet. After more than two years, all the patients had maintained the low levels of triglycerides. The general trend observed with the lowering of cholesterol was also observed in triglyceride levels. The older the individuals, the less rapid the decrease in triglyceride levels. However, all patients had a significant reduction in triglyceride levels.

The reason for the decrease in cholesterol levels is really not so surprising. Cholesterol biosynthesis is known to be suppressed by the intake of cholesterol in the diet.[24] This means that if cholesterol is consumed in the diet, the body will not make cholesterol from other substances. Perhaps what is observed is that if dietary cholesterol is reduced too low, the body responds by making too much of it. How many of you have high cholesterol levels, even though you eat virtually no animal fats? Unfortunately, dramatic decreases in cholesterol from a low-carbohydrate diet are further out of reach the longer one has been eating too many carbohydrates. However, you can see from Figure 6.5 that cholesterol levels do not continue to rise either. As we have said before, cholesterol levels in the blood are a poor marker for heart disease. There is plenty of evidence that even suggests, on the contrary, that high cholesterol levels increase health.

THE CARBOHYDRATE THEORY
OF ARTERIOSCLEROSIS

Obviously, the chapter about human arteriosclerosis has to be rewritten. We have shown you a small part of the vast amounts of evidence that indicate the fat theory has failed. But there is an alternative to the fat theory.[25] The carbohydrate theory of arteriosclerosis follows the idea that the primary factor associated with the disease is tissue damage to the arterial walls. The tissue damage theory was proposed by German[26] and American[27] researchers. This damage comes from the overproduction of catabolic hormones such as thyroid hormones and cortisone, which stimulate the breakdown of tissue, not its repair. It is the slow erosion of the inner arterial tissue from too much catabolic breakdown that is the cause of arteriosclerosis, just as it is also a cause of other health problems. Coupled with this catabolism is the decreased level of growth hormone. Both of these factors are the primary events that lead to heart disease from the overconsumption of carbohydrates. Any lipids present in these damaged sections of artery are only there as a secondary event. They might tend to "precipitate" out of the blood because of the changes in the surface of the damaged tissue, or they might actually be associated with the repair of the tissue. Of course, there are many subtleties and biochemical processes that ultimately go wrong, but the carbohydrate hypothesis explains much more of the available information then does cholesterol alone. The next section will show you just how powerful high-fat, low-carbohydrate diets can be for repairing your heart.

CARDIAC FAILURE

Unfortunately, many heart disease problems are actually problems with the heart itself—an enlarged heart, insufficient energy to maintain a steady beat, or a heart valve problem. *Cardiopathy* is the general term given to diseases of the heart. These conditions also respond favorably to low-carbohydrate nutrition.

In 1958, Dr. Lutz treated a thirty-five-year-old woman who had severely elevated blood pressure, kidney disease, and associated retinopathy (this is an inflammation of the retina usually caused from high blood pressure). She had been released from the hospital in order to die at home because all conventional treatments at that time had failed. Dr. Lutz treated her with restriction of carbohydrates and salt. The success achieved by dietary restriction of carbohydrates surpassed all expectations.

His other heart patients were then treated with low-carbohydrate nutrition. In two of the early cases, heart valve defects were treated successfully. One man has continued his low-carbohydrate nutrition, and after ten years the initial symptoms of a loud heart murmur and a dilation of the left atrium are no longer observed. The man works again in a quarry. A female patient whose aortic valve would not close and experienced shortness of breath and palpitations had a good recovery after just a few months on the diet.

In all of these people and others, the abnormal electrocardiograms (ECGs) became much more normal after low-carbohydrate nutrition. An ECG is the measurement of the electrical signals the heart receives to make it beat. To support all our statements with evidence, we have put together the ECGs of seven different cases of heart patients before and after a low-carbohydrate diet was adopted. These are shown in Figure 6.6. There are many leads attached to a person to evaluate the ECG. In Figure 6.6, we show only leads 1 and V_5. Even if you do not understand these results, you can still see that there are changes between the "before" and "after" ECGs, and you can take our word that the "after" is much better than the "before."

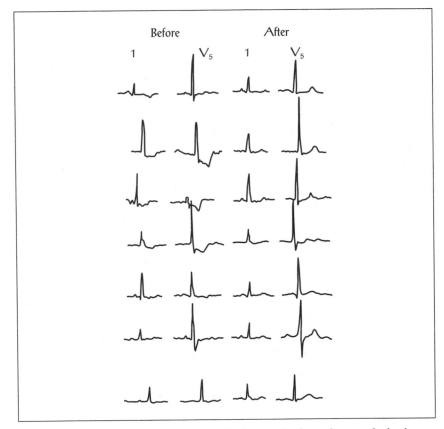

Figure 6.6 ECGs from some patients before and after a low-carbohydrate diet. The amelioration from low-carbohydrate nutrition is striking.

Even though there was much success in treating many people with heart problems, some conditions worsened before they got better. After adopting low-carbohydrate nutrition, one twenty-eight-year-old patient who was suffering from mitral stenosis (a cardiac valve defect) had some problems. His heart enlarged and edema developed in the right thorax. After a while, his condition improved beyond the initial problem. Figure 6.7 shows four X-rays of this man's chest region. The white areas represent the enlargement of

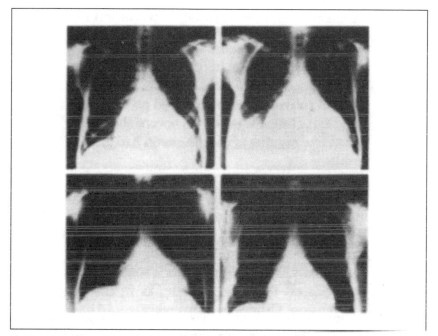

Figure 6.7 These four X-rays (from upper left to lower right) of a twenty-eight-year-old patient suffering from mitral stenosis (a cardiac valve defect) demonstrate how the heart first enlarged and edema developed in the right thorax. Later on, everything went well.

the heart and fluid retention. You can see that the low-carbohydrate diet helped return this man's heart to a more normal state. Compare the top left X-ray (before) with the lower right one (after). The top right X-ray shows that initially there was an increase in edema and enlargement of the heart (more white areas) before there was improvement. This case represents an immune form of heart failure. This patient required an initial suppression of the immune system using gold salts, which are used in other autoimmune diseases. Here again it was found that initially the immune system required "taming" in order to achieve the beneficial result. Many operations for heart replacement could be eliminated if this conservative method would be developed properly and used by cardiologists.

SUMMARY

In this chapter, we have evaluated the original epidemiological studies designed to prove that animal fats in the diet are the promoting factor for arteriosclerosis. Clearly, these studies were poorly interpreted and should never have been so readily molded into the framework of the fat theory. Today, new evidence indicates that fat is not a significant heart disease problem.

New epidemiological studies by researchers at Harvard University are showing that fat is not only benign with relation to heart disease but suggests there may be a benefit from fat in the diet.

We also have shown that protein in the diet is beneficial. Of course, this must be true—our bodies are made up of protein. The promoters of low-protein diets remain oblivious to many factors, but most important is that no amount of supplementation can substitute for the balance of fat and protein that is obtained from animal foods, the way nature intended.

However, we do not promote a protein-only diet: Fat must be included. The most prevalent argument against high protein in the diet is that kidney function can be compromised. This is probably a reference to data published many years ago, which indicated if someone already has a kidney disease, then amino acids can exacerbate the condition. Nowhere have we found any evidence that kidney function suffers from a low-carbohydrate diet. On the contrary, as we have shown by direct measurements on people, uric acid in the blood decreases when low-carbohydrate diets are employed. Furthermore, recent studies indicate no benefit of a low-protein diet for children who have an existing kidney disease.[28]

We have also presented one alternate theory of heart disease. Homocysteine is now accepted worldwide as a major risk factor in heart disease. Three vitamins, B_6, B_{12}, and folic acid, all of which are in poor supply under a high-carbohydrate, low-fat diet, are crucial for maintaining low levels of homocysteine in the blood.

Along with this information, the evidence presented in this chapter also comes from one author's own work. Dr. Lutz's experiences with thousands of patients are powerful evidence in support of low-carbohydrate nutrition to reduce heart disease and, as we have seen up to now, many other metabolic problems associated with diet. Those who disagree must prove otherwise. If there are any data that show all positive results of a low-fat, high-carbohydrate diet on triglycerides, uric acid, cholesterol, blood pressure, and cardiac output in people who have existing diseases over a two- to three-year period, we'd like to see it!

CHAPTER SEVEN

Gastrointestinal Disorders: Reduction, Relief, and Restoration

PROBLEMS ASSOCIATED WITH THE STOMACH and intestines are very common but are not discussed very often in books or in the media. Yet they have affected all of us at one time or another. They are generally more of a nuisance than life threatening, yet some of the top-selling pharmaceutical drugs are for heartburn relief. There also are many over-the-counter products for sale that promise to bring relief to gastrointestinal disorders. Probably most of them work. But are they necessary?

The prevailing theme surrounding gastrointestinal disorders is that fat and meat in the diet cause most of the problems, yet there is little evidence of this. Fat has been given a bad rap here because of the "overlap phenomenon": Ever since fat was proposed to be the dietary factor that contributed to heart disease, many other ailments have been assumed to be associated with fat in the diet. This is considered to be true even for cancer, although most of the available evidence suggests otherwise. When people eat fatty meals, they sometimes observe gastrointestinal problems. But what else is there in that meal? How much food did they eat? We're willing to bet that there are plenty of carbohydrates, too.

What we will show you in this chapter is that there is a profound influence on the gut when a low-carbohydrate diet is adopted, and it is a good influence. As with most of our degenerative diseases, gastrointestinal diseases are associated with long-term influence from the diet. Some of the more severe diseases, such as ulcerative colitis and Crohn's disease, can require years on a low-carbohydrate diet to go into a stable remission state.

The benefits of reducing carbohydrates can be observed on such simple problems such as stomach pain after eating. Most of the gas associated with food comes from the by-products of fermentation of sugars from the intestinal bacteria. (Remember that fermentation is the process that bacteria use to generate energy in the absence of oxygen; this was presented in chapter 5.) Since the gastrointestinal tract contains intestinal flora—the symbiotic bacteria that reside in the gut and benefit the body—it is at the front line of the body's response to food. A reduction in carbohydrates leads almost immediately to reduced gas formation and, therefore, less discomfort on a day-to-day basis. The introduction of a low-carbohydrate diet as a general mode of therapy for disorders of this system is therefore logical, albeit contrary to what has been practiced.

A reduction of carbohydrates in the diet not only provides relief for simple irritations, but also can return a gastrointestinal system compromised by serious disease to a normal state. Although this diet is not universally beneficial for all gastrointestinal problems, many digestive problems are eliminated by it.

GASTRIC DISORDERS

Because fat in the diet has been thought to evoke unpleasant symptoms in many patients, the opinion has arisen that a gastric diet has to be low in fat. But a low-fat diet never brings about a cure. Those of you who have had these symptoms are well aware that a reduction in dietary fat did not give much relief. For most simple gastric disorders, a low-carbohydrate diet is all that is needed to bring complete relief. Patients feel distinctly better even within a few days and usually are completely well again within a couple of weeks. But if they again begin to eat too many carbohydrates, they quickly notice that these were responsible for their discomfort, not the fat or other foods.

Too Much Acid

Distressing heartburn often is the first symptom to disappear following withdrawal of carbohydrates from the diet. This has been observed in hundreds of people. It has not been measured scientifically, however, since only the person with the problem will know if it has dissipated.

Often, patients have come back to Dr. Lutz and complained that the low-carbohydrate diet is no longer effective and their heartburn has returned. But a closer look usually reveals that too many carbohydrates have again crept into the diet. Dr. Allan also has found that people who have gone on the low-carbohydrate diet observe an immediate improvement in heartburn and stomach pain after eating if they experienced these problems on their old diet.

In some way, carbohydrates appear to disturb acid regulation. The normal state of affairs is that acid is produced by the stomach when it has something to digest; only a "sick" stomach produces digestive juices when empty. This so-called "fasting secretion" is the reason for the autodigestion seen in gastric ulcers. Excess gastric acid is responsible for, or provides the right conditions for, development of a gastric ulcer, which is deducible from the fact that a typical gastric ulcer is found only in sites where contact with gastric juice is possible.

Gastritis and Ulcers

Gastritis and many types of ulcers will heal if carbohydrates are restricted in the diet of the affected person. Gastritis is an inflammation of the stomach, especially the mucous lining. Ulcers are similar to gastritis, but are usually small lesions of the stomach lining. Hyperacidity (acid reflux) and heartburn, as it is called, can be eliminated by carbohydrate restriction, as can duodenal ulcers. These ulcers are found in the first part of the small intestine, which is called the *duodenum*. Some ulcers are known to be caused by the bacterium *Helicobacter pylori*. These are treated successfully with antibiotics. A diet with too much carbohydrate means a diet with too little fat. There are numerous fats known to be powerful antimicrobial agents. Low-fat diets may promote microbial growth in the stomach and intestines. For this reason, it is reasonable to conclude that stomach infections with *Helicobacter pylori* could be reduced under the influence of a low-carbohydrate diet.

Other ulcers, however, such as the callous gastric ulcer, should not be treated immediately by simple restriction of carbohydrates. These ulcers are stress-induced. Transition to a new diet entails further stress. Callous gastric ulcers should be treated with small doses of cortisone until they disappear, and then a low-carbohydrate diet should be slowly introduced.

Why Do Carbohydrates Cause Stomach Problems?

We have already mentioned that simple problems such as gas and bloating are a result of the fermentation of carbohydrates by intestinal flora. This is an interesting side point to a much more important explanation of exactly how carbohydrates exert their influence in the stomach. Just like other disorders of metabolism associated with carbohydrates, stomach problems are a consequence of hormonal excess.

Excess insulin production from dietary carbohydrates can overstimulate the pancreas, which can lead to the overproduction of gastrin. Gastrin is the polypeptide secretion hormone of the stomach that causes the production of acid. Excess gastrin production results in too much stomach acid, and therefore, ulcers, hyperacidity, acid reflux, and other common complaints in some people.

Because gastrin is made in the pancreatic duct, the same region of the stomach where insulin is produced, Dr. Lutz calls this condition the *pancreatic duct syndrome*. Many pancreatic hormones can also be released into the stomach by overstimulation of the pancreas. For example, the hormone serotonin is responsible for hot flashes and headaches after a meal. These symptoms disappear immediately when patients adopt low-carbohydrate nutrition. Therefore, one must conclude that overstimulation of the pancreas by the constant need to produce insulin results in the secretion of other pancreatic hormones. The pancreatic duct syndrome explains virtually all the familiar complaints from people with gastrointestinal problems.

COLON DISORDERS

Constipation and Diarrhea

On the whole, constipation is the most common illness of the colon. Billions of dollars are spent on laxatives, but these do not heal the problem—they only give temporary relief. The effects of laxatives usually diminish with time so that the dosage has to be increased or the preparation has to be changed. In the long run, laxatives are detrimental to your health because they cause an evacuation of the bowel by irritating it, and because they disturb the mineral metabolism (causing loss of potassium). This constant irritation of the mucosa finally leads to the most predominant complaint among chronically constipated patients: They feel constipated although their colon is totally empty.

When people begin a low-carbohydrate diet, the stool becomes more solid and temporary constipation can result. Low-carbohydrate diets usually are initially accompanied by some loss of water weight. (Contrary to what is said about this, it is not a bad thing. Some of you probably already take medication to reduce your water weight.) The consumption of water should follow the body's signals: If you are thirsty, drink water; if not, don't drink water. Contrary to popular beliefs, too much water (or other fluids) may dilute enzymes in the entera and also make the kidneys work harder. So drink as needed.

In the beginning of a low-carbohydrate diet, people who are already chronically constipated do not do well with just a reduction in carbohydrates. Generally, a daily cleansing enema with 1½ liters of warm water without additives will help the transition into the low-carbohydrate diet. Under the continued diet, the stool eventually will normalize. In children, this can take one or two days; in young adults, one or two weeks; and in older persons, a few months, but undoubtedly, as has been observed in hundreds of people from Dr. Lutz's practice, the evacuation process will normalize. The problem here is that the muscles responsible for pushing the stool through the digestive system become weak in high-carbohydrate eaters because excess carbohydrates tend to "poison" the gut, which increases bowel movements without the need for muscle action. Adoption of a low-carbohydrate diet eventually will strengthen the muscles, but some time may be necessary.

Chronic diarrhea, which is much more common than generally assumed, can be treated successfully with a low-carbohydrate diet. Some people have had diarrhea for years and have become so used to it that they no longer perceive their condition as unusual. Although there are differences in the time required to return the stool to normal, chronic diarrhea has always disappeared in Dr. Lutz's patients with a low-carbohydrate diet.

Diverticulosis

The wall of the colon consists of several muscle layers that cross each other and, like a lattice, leave small open spaces through which blood vessels and nerves can pass. When these muscle layers weaken, the spaces enlarge to the point that mucosa can protrude through the meshwork. These fingerlike mucosa protrusions get under the peritoneum covering most of the colon and become deformed into button shapes. These "buttons" are covered by the peritoneum on the outside and, therefore, are fixed in place and can no longer retract. On the inside, they contain stool or other bowel contents.

The number of these "diverticula" can vary greatly. Some people have one or two diverticula and others have twenty to fifty. These diverticula generally do not cause symptoms unless they become inflamed, but the resulting peritonitis can, at times, necessitate immediate surgery. The diverticula are most commonly localized in an area of the large bowel called the *sigmoid colon,* an S-shaped loop between the rectum and descending colon on the left side. Inflammation here creates symptoms just as appendicitis would create symptoms on the right side.

Because scientists observed years ago that Africans who ate fiber-rich diets had no diverticulosis and also fewer other colon diseases (such as cancer), a diet rich in fibers is recommended for the treatment of diverticulosis. We will talk much more about fiber and its relation to colon cancer in chapter 10.

For now, suffice it to say that we do not believe the fiber hypothesis has been proven. However, it is a theory that has become very popular over the last few years, due in large part to people who publish simply what they read in other lay publications: Someone reads an article in a health magazine, and the next thing you know they're an "expert author" on the same topic.

The problem with high-fiber diets is that they almost always include large amounts of carbohydrates. The truth is that most foods marketed as high-fiber foods—cereals, breads, and fruit—are high in carbohydrates and actually quite low in fiber. In order to get the recommended amount of fiber, you would have to eat a large amount of these high-carbohydrate foods. Fiber, by definition, is material that is not digested, so in theory it should contain very little carbohydrate. True fiber would be something like raw wheat bran, which is stripped from the wheat berry before it is used in today's mass-produced foods. Other high-fiber, low-carbohydrate foods are broccoli, cauliflower, celery, lettuce, and nuts.

Dr. Lutz found that diverticulosis could be treated very successfully with a low-carbohydrate diet. This can still be a high-fiber diet since the truly high-fiber foods mentioned above are actually low in carbohydrates. In cases of diverticulosis, the prevention of initial constipation through the regular application of cleansing enemas is particularly important. After a few months, there will be normal stools and no further complaints relating to diverticulosis. The existing diverticula will not disappear, but no new ones will form. Most importantly, the in-flammation, which very often exists in the gastrointestinal canal of people on normal diets, and which spreads to the diverticula, will heal. Finally, the bowel musculature will strengthen and the original cause of the diverticula, namely the muscular weakness with the enlarged spaces between the bundles, disappears.

Crohn's Disease

Crohn's disease is a severe form of enterocolitis. It was named after the American physician Burril Crohn, who was the first to show that the tumorlike swelling in Crohn's disease was inflammatory and not cancerous.[1] In Crohn's disease, the illness is not limited to the mucosa alone, as in enterocolitis, but instead involves all levels of the bowel, the mesentery, the lymph nodes, the gallbladder, the duodenum, and the stomach. The main site of Crohn's disease is the last part of the small bowel, but it can extend into the colon.

Crohn's disease has become much more common in recent years. In the last ten years, more than 600 cases have been observed and treated in Dr. Lutz's practice.

The distinction between Crohn's disease and ulcerative colitis is significant. Crohn's disease, in contrast to ulcerative colitis, heals with great probability from a low-carbohydrate diet within six months to one year, and usually without complications. Those afflicted with these very similar colon disorders would be advised to be sure their doctors have made the correct diagnosis because Crohn's disease is readily treated with carbohydrate restriction, whereas ulcerative colitis takes more time and there are relapses even if the patient adheres strictly to the 6 BU (bread unit) diet. In ulcerative colitis, there is always some bleeding. The involvement of the colon observed using endoscopy decreases from the end to the beginning of the colon. In Crohn's disease, the most-often-involved part is the end of the intestine, and from there the beginning of the colon. In ulcerative colitis, the process is always limited to the mucosa, whereas in Crohn's, the muscular layers and the lymph vessels are involved. This can lead to fistulas and other complications, which necessitate surgery.

Crohn's disease is still regarded as incurable by Western medicine. This is because the simple concept of reducing carbohydrates in the diet is not included in the treatment arsenal of modern medicine. There was some discussion in the scientific literature years ago about the benefit of reducing refined sugar and flour for the treatment of Crohn's disease.[2,3] Dr. Lutz was the only one to follow this up. However, he went even further and prescribed a treatment regimen of a reduction of total carbohydrates, not just refined, processed carbohydrates.[4]

While a low-carbohydrate diet does not provide a cure rate of 100 percent there is a high rate of return to normalcy without a relapse, which is as close to a cure as one can get today. We hope that the results we are about to show will change the current treatment of Crohn's disease. It is certainly a shame that so many suffer when a simple treatment is available, and one that bears no great medication cost.

The results obtained from sixty-seven patients with Crohn's disease who were treated with carbohydrate restriction are shown in Figure 7.1. Patients were followed for up to three years to determine the long-term effects of carbohydrate restriction on their disease. More than 80 percent of the patients were symptom-free after eighteen months on the diet, and 70 percent were symptom-free after six months on the diet.

We have included in this figure a line representing the failures— those who did not respond to the diet. Unfortunately, the low-carbohydrate diet does not cure everyone afflicted with Crohn's disease, but it still offers the best clinical outcome that we have ever observed for these people. We know that some people stop the low-carbohydrate program after a few months because they see no improvement, or their doctor disapproves of the diet. Sometimes the complications are too severe and prevent a rapid amelioration. In any event, the failures might simply be due to stopping the diet.

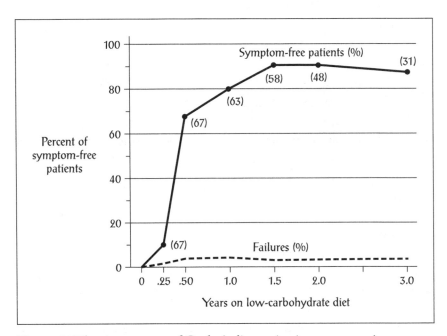

Figure 7.1 The time course of Crohn's disease in sixty-seven patients (initially) who followed a low-carbohydrate diet. After one-and-a-half years, over 80 percent were symptom-free. The numbers in parentheses are the total number of patients evaluated at the given time.

The most easily measured parameters used to monitor the course of Crohn's disease are blood iron levels. Typically, these levels are below normal in Crohn's patients. A return to normal levels is a good marker that the problem has disappeared, in addition to how the patients feel and how their physical symptoms regress. Figure 7.2 shows what happens to the iron count in the blood serum over the course of three years in Crohn's patients who adopted a low-carbohydrate diet. There is an initial decrease in already below-normal levels after about three months, but the levels steadily rise and normalize after eight months on the diet. This also corresponds to the changes in physical symptoms that these patients experienced, shown in Figure 7.1.

In a more controlled study of Crohn's disease, a reduction of carbohydrates also resulted in significant improvement compared to

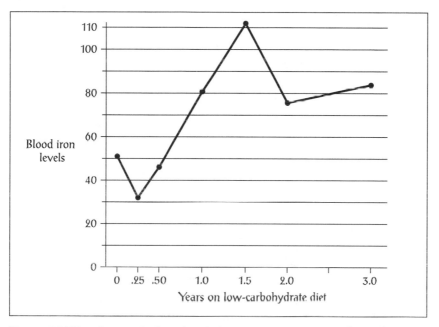

Figure 7.2 The changes in iron levels improve in patients with Crohn's disease when a low-carbohydrate (72 g/24 hour) diet is adopted.

patients who did not use the diet. A prospective, randomized study of the effects of a reduction of carbohydrates was done with the co-operation of the German Morbus Crohn and Ulcerative Colitis Association.[5] Two groups of fifty voluntary patients were chosen who were undergoing inpatient treatment of large doses of cortisone at the beginning of the study. Cortisone is a steroid that can reduce autoimmune reactions and inflammation, and is used as a treatment for many types of autoimmune disorders. Long-term use of steroids is damaging to the body, and alternate therapy is always desirable.

The study design was such that, in both the control group—those who did not eat a low-carbohydrate diet—and the intervention group—those who were supposed to adopt a low-carbohydrate diet of 72 grams or less in twenty-four hours—the cortisone medication was stopped. Participants were monitored and evaluated to determine the rate of relapse of their Crohn's symptoms. In reality, most

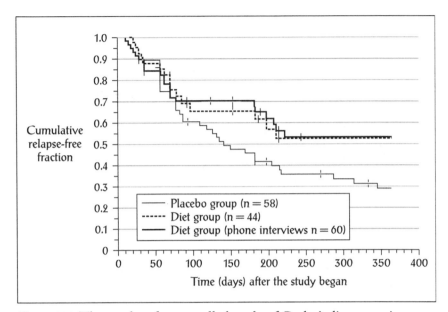

Figure 7.3 The results of a controlled study of Crohn's disease patients. After stopping treatment with cortisone, one group adopted a low-carbohydrate diet , and the other did not. After 90 days, more relapses were observed with the control (placebo) group. After 200 days on the low-carbohydrate diet, there were no more relapses, whereas in the control group relapses continued. Each relapse made the curves move lower.

of the low-carbohydrate group did not stick with the 72 grams per day. They consumed up to 12 BUs per day, or 150 grams of carbohydrate. The results of this study are presented in Figure 7.3. Even though the intake of carbohydrates was greater than what Dr. Lutz had required of his patients, the results were impressive. After 90 days, the patients on the diet had already started to see differences, compared to the control group. Relapses were clearly less frequent in the diet group; after 200 days, the diet group experienced no more relapses at all. The end result was that patients who were treated with a reduction of carbohydrates had their symptoms essentially disappear.

Once again we see that the influence of a reduction of carbohydrates plays a key role in a health benefit. Fat is not the culprit here, nor is fat the culprit in most other age-related degenerative diseases. The time has certainly come to return to the diet that mankind evolved to eat, and to set the human race on a steady course to eliminating many of today's "incurable" diseases.

Ulcerative Colitis

Ulcerative colitis may begin one day quite harmlessly with the appearance of blood in the stool. The physician diagnoses hemorrhoids, but they cannot be found with the rectoscope. Then the physician sees a reddened mucosa, which starts bleeding at the slightest touch. In mild cases, this process is restricted to the rectum; the more severe the disease, the further it extends upward. In contrast to Crohn's disease, the small intestine, the gallbladder, the duodenum, and the stomach are never involved in ulcerative colitis; only the mucosa and the underlying muscle layers are affected. In time, however, both are destroyed to an extent that the whole colon contracts into a short cylinder that is completely motionless and has lost most of its function.

Ulcerative colitis becomes life-threatening either when it turns into a condition called *toxic megacolon*, or when malignant degeneration, or cancer of the colon, begins. A toxic megacolon can develop at any time as long as the ulcerative colitis is active. The final stage of these conditions is surgical removal of the entire colon.

Even though ulcerative colitis responds to low-carbohydrate nutrition, its course is not as rapid as that of Crohn's disease. However, very positive results have been observed using the low-carbohydrate diet for ulcerative colitis patients.[6–10]

In all, more than 600 of Dr. Lutz's gastrointestinal patients have been treated with low-carbohydrate nutrition. Many patients came to Dr. Lutz from hospitals where they were told, "There is no diet

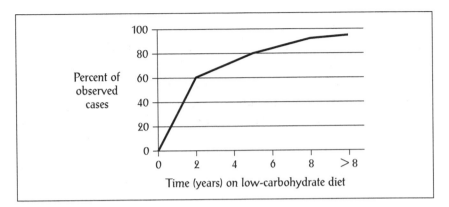

Figure 7.4 The progress of seventy-four patients with ulcerative colitis after adopting a low-carbohytdrate (72g/24 hours) diet. The line in the graph represents the percent of patients who had no symptoms. After two years, 60 percent of the patients had no symptoms. But it takes almost eight years to see 90 percent without symptoms.

for ulcerative colitis or Crohn's disease. Eat whatever you can tolerate. Take your medication and come back to us when you have a relapse. Eventually you may have to be operated on anyway."

Out of a total of 285 ulcerative colitis patients treated in Dr. Lutz's practice through 1984, only 3 have since died. One was a relatively young man who had recovered quite well under a low-carbohydrate diet and had gained 40 pounds. Suddenly he became acutely ill with high fever and abdominal pain. He was admitted to a clinic but was operated on too late because he had fiercely refused this operation. Another patient underwent surgery without approval; the third, a very elderly lady, died two months after an operation for thromboembolism.

Of the first seventy-four patients treated until 1979 with a low-carbohydrate diet, approximately 60 percent were without complaints after two years. They had normal laboratory values and normal rectal mucosa. The remaining 40 percent took longer to stabilize. Some of these patients required up to eight years until the bleeding stopped, iron levels normalized, and diarrhea and abdominal pain subsided. Figure 7.4 shows a graphic depiction of how patients responded to a low-carbohydrate diet. These patients were followed for eight years, which represents an unprecedented length of time relative to most studies. It took two years to see that 60 percent of the patients had been symptom free, and improvement is still observed at the eight-year mark. In all of the studies we present throughout this book, ulcerative colitis required the longest time on a low-carbohydrate diet to observe the benefit.

Certainly, this is not an easy form of therapy. It requires cooperation and sacrifice from the patient, patience from the physician, and time. Whoever believes they can get rid of their colitis in a few months is mistaken. But one has to see the success of the diet in relation to its alternatives; there are none we know of that can give these overall results.

Relapses

In contrast to Crohn's disease, even after the resolution of ulcerative colitis there can be a relapse. From year to year, these relapses become less probable and less severe. The recurrent disease is usually mild and lasts only a few months.

Ulcerative colitis is distinctly a disease of the immune system. The immune system does not forget if it ever has been sensitized to the body's own organs. The words of Professor Ludwig Demling, a specialist of gastrointestinal diseases, still hold true: "Once colitis, always colitis." Demling meant this in a different context, namely that once a person had ulcerative colitis, they would never get rid of the disease. But this theory changes under a low-carbohydrate diet. Once a person has colitis, their immune system will remain primed toward the colon, but the colon becomes more resistant and can cope better with the immune system's attacks. After a while, the immune system loses interest in such attacks. Because the colon does not react to the attacks, the immune system is less stimulated and its reactions are less intense.

Chicken pox is a good example of the immune system reacting to the body: Most people contract chicken pox during childhood. Some develop a typical rash, others just have fever, but most children do get the disease. With increasing age, the immunity against this pathogen wears off, so that a person can be infected with chicken pox again. This time the infection manifests itself in the form of shingles. Sometimes this reinfection can be very extensive; however, usually it passes without fever and is restricted to small areas of the skin. In a similar way, the body's immune system reacts less harshly to later bouts of colitis.

Malignancy

Malignant degeneration (i.e., the development of colon cancer) is another danger faced by a patient with ulcerative colitis. Usually it takes ten to fifteen years for a cancer to develop; often, these patients have had their colitis since their youth, and the cancer develops at multiple sites. Whether or not patients who have been on a low-carbohydrate diet develop colon cancer, we cannot say.

Among Dr. Lutz's first 100 patients, 2 had cancer. One woman simultaneously had leukemia, a malignant blood disease, and colon cancer.

The second case was an older man. After he had been well for over a decade, hemorrhages recurred. A suspicious area in his colon was found, but a biopsy taken at that site was negative. Eventually he was operated on anyway, and cancer was found. The surgeon said later that he had not found any indication of ulcerative colitis in the colon. After more than ten years of a low-carbohydrate diet, the disease had essentially disappeared. Postoperatively, the patient started to eat everything again, only to return with a relapse of his colitis. Today his surgeon prescribes a low-carbohydrate diet for colitis patients in his hospital.

WHY DOES LOW-CARBOHYDRATE NUTRITION WORK?

We do not know exactly why low-carbohydrate nutrition has such an impressive effect in the treatment of Crohn's disease and colitis. But we can speculate based on the basic premise of why carbohydrate restriction helps in many diseases. Our idea here is that carbohydrates induce the pancreas, specifically the islet cells, into overstimulation, that is, excess insulin production. This is a known fact. This overstimulation may radiate to the other islet cells, which causes the entera to accelerate the movement of ingested food, so that the intestine cannot digest them properly. This partially undigested food enters the terminal ileum, which is not able to absorb the foodstuffs. Eventually, the undigested food enters the colon where the bacteria there digest it, which causes chronic irritation, involvement of the immune system, and colitis.

This is the same way that hyperacidity is caused by too much carbohydrate in the diet. Gastrin, the hormone that gives rise to acid production in the stomach, is a close relative to the insulin-producing islet cells. Overstimulation of the islet cells for insulin production may result in overstimulation of other similar cells.

MEDICATION

Medications cannot be discontinued immediately since it takes some time for the diet to take effect. First, the patient should be weaned from cortisone since these artificial adrenal cortex preparations generally inhibit protein synthesis. This means they not only suppress the production of immune cells and thereby subdue the symptoms, but they also interfere with the healing of the mucosa. Eventually the patient will be able to discontinue all medications. Should there be a relapse in the first few years, one can temporarily take up the medication again. A mild relapse does not require medication.

Dr. Lutz has a large file full of thank-you letters from patients who had tried every possible therapy unsuccessfully and finally were left with surgery as the only option, before they came to him. There are more than fifty thousand cases of Crohn's disease and ulcerative colitis in the German-speaking countries alone, and surely at least that many in the United States. We ask, "Why aren't these sufferers put on a low-carbohydrate diet? Why doesn't this simple treatment become established?"

Perhaps it is because the results we have just presented are not known. We fear, however, that there is no limit to the disdain of those who practice orthodox medicine for all alternative, "outsider" treatment methods—acupuncture, neural therapy, chiropractic, homeopathy, to name but a few. We agree that caution is partially justified, but no one used their orthodox medicine to prove the alternatives wrong!

We find that this is where many problems arise with today's "medicine." Techniques that show promise, or methods such as low-carbohydrate nutrition that have been proven, are generally ignored—not disproved, just ignored. A well-known and respected researcher simply has to say that a method does not work, and bingo! Without any proof, an unsubstantiated statement then becomes the dogma of the day. But this situation is changing. To ignore scientific information, is, in our opinion, irresponsible. There is, however, a viable alternative: Eat what you can tolerate.

SUMMARY

Although colon and gastrointestinal disorders are not often considered when people talk about diseases, both represent significant problems for a great many people. We have shown you that serious diseases of the digestive tract show great improvement when a low-carbohydrate diet is the chosen food regimen.

As we indicate throughout this book, low-carbohydrate nutrition actually can correct many poor-health conditions; therefore, it must be the correct diet adapted by human physiology. Nowhere in the scientific literature has a comprehensive set of data been formulated to indicate that a low-fat diet can resolve so many conditions. We absolutely believe that most of the diseases we discuss would never even begin if people maintained a low-carbohydrate diet throughout their lifetime.

It is time to move past the special interests that guide today's low-fat food craze and face the facts. Whether it's the carbohydrate producers or the people who can't or won't admit that their theory has failed, it is time to think of the greater good for humankind. Those who state that low-carbohydrate diets are a "fad" are either in denial, ignoring the facts, or aren't thinking clearly about it.

Carbohydrates, particularly in large amounts, are the most recent, as well as the most harmful, addition to the human diet. All you have to do is follow the program outlined in this book, and after a few months you, too, will know the truth. And when you feel that good, no one will be able to convince you that you're doing something detrimental to your health.

CHAPTER EIGHT

Weight Control

IN AMERICAN CULTURE, NOTHING promotes heated discussion more than the topic of a person's weight. And no wonder. In the last twenty years, there has been an incredible increase in the number of people who are considered overweight and obese. Estimates in a recent article in *Science* suggested that 54 percent of all adults in the United States are overweight, and more than 25 percent of American children are overweight or obese. For children, this number represents a 40 percent increase in the last sixteen years. And unfortunately, all indications are that this trend will continue.

Why has this happened? What is the first thing that comes to your mind when you think of gaining weight or trying to lose it? FAT. For the past forty or more years, we have been told that fat is the big issue in weight control, and foods, menus, and diets have reflected this belief. Yet obesity and overweight numbers are on a rapid rise. So what do most of the "experts" say?

"Reduce fat intake even further. Eat more fruits and vegetables and grains, preferably whole grains. Avoid red meat and choose a salad with a low-fat dressing instead. Eat bagels instead of cake, breakfast cereal instead of eggs."

Well, Americans *have* been eating this way, and guess what! It's not working. Even so, it will take time for the public to understand that carbohydrates are the main cause of this problem and so many others—but the tide will eventually turn because it is clear that the low-fat theory just hasn't worked.

The number of obese, overweight, and diabetic people is dangerously close to an epidemic, even though people have been operating under the low-fat mode for years, and the main reason is that low-fat diets contain so much carbohydrate that insulin resistance, hyperinsulinemia, and Type 2 diabetes have skyrocketed. Human physiology has not adapted to such a large intake of carbohydrates. This has been proven throughout this book.

Time and time again, we have shown you that people either are cured or react positively when they adopt a low-carbohydrate diet to battle the diseases of civilization. This realization should prove that the low-fat concept of nutrition has failed. Yet most people will interpret the increase in numbers of overweight people as proof that Americans need to decrease dietary fat even further. What will they say when people at last are eating zero fat and still getting sicker? (By that time, the public may be urged to achieve negative fat intake—perhaps an "anti-fat" pill will have been invented to assist in the endeavor.)

It goes without saying that exercise is also a very important factor in health and weight management; unfortunately, the general American public is moving toward less exercise. That's just the way it is, and our health officials need to approach the problem realistically. Even studies on exercise have revealed that exercise alone is often not sufficient to promote proper metabolic balance. The correct nutrition will not only control weight, but it should also increase the desire and ability to exercise. A low-fat diet does just the opposite. It weakens muscles and lowers energy, so exercise becomes more difficult.

LOW-CARBOHYDRATE DIETS

We have waited until this stage of the book to discuss weight control because the focus on weight control alone tends to obscure the more important concepts and factors of overall health and disease. We have shown that a reduction of carbohydrates to 72 grams or less per day resulted in many long-term benefits for people who already had some metabolic disease other than being overweight. For many of the people who've been part of the data we have shown in graphs, weight loss was a natural outcome from a reduction in carbohydrates in their diet.

A low-carbohydrate diet has been rediscovered by physicians in both Great Britain and the United States as a means of losing weight.[1-3] The title of Herman Taller's best-seller *Calories Don't Count*[4] suggests that it is unnecessary to starve in order to slim; the author writes that success can often be achieved without lowering the intake of calories, if carbohydrates are reduced instead. Dr. Atkins's *Diet Revolution*[5] sparked a renewed interest in low-carbohydrate nutrition as a means to successfully lose weight. The success of all Dr. Atkins's books proves that the diet does indeed work; those who follow it do lose weight.

The "Astronaut's Diet," a low-carbohydrate diet, has recently been introduced into the U.S. Air Force in order to prevent pilots from becoming too heavy. There are other important reasons for giving pilots and astronauts a low-carbohydrate diet: It prevents flatulence, stomach pains, and the production of intestinal gases that become troublesome when flying at high altitudes or in a space capsule with its reduced air pressure.

The Drinking Man's Diet[6] gained much attention when published in 1965. Instead of struggling to abstain from alcohol altogether, the authors recommended instead abstinence from carbohydrates. They described how this would make it possible to drink more freely while avoiding the usual unpleasant consequences. We do not, however, recommend this theory, since alcohol is not simply carbohydrate. Its breakdown via acetaldehyde indicates a similarity to the fatty acids, and it undeniably has a toxic effect on brain and liver cells. But it is true that a reduction of carbohydrates will tend to benefit the heavy drinker, as long as sufficient amounts of protein and fat are consumed.

THE "POINT" DIET

The low-carbohydrate diet surfaced in Europe in 1968 when Austrian author Erna Carise summed up the main facts in a small booklet entitled *Punkte-Diät* (Point-Diet).[7]

In this program, 1 gram of carbohydrate is taken as equivalent to 1 point, and the book lists the number of points contained in various foodstuffs. For example, a bread roll contains the equivalent of about 25 grams of carbohydrate and thus is allocated 25 points; a potato weighing 60 grams contains 12 grams of carbohydrate and rates 12 points. This diet permitted 60 points or grams of carbohydrates per day.

This small book was a popular sensation in the German-speaking countries, and about 400,000 copies have been sold to date.

WHAT ARE WE EATING THESE DAYS?

Everyone who has tried a low-carbohydrate diet to lose weight knows that it's the best way to lose weight out of all the weight-loss programs currently available. Many of you also know that even if you reduce your total calories, particularly fat calories, you often still do not lose weight, and sometimes you even continue to gain weight. This is because eating carbohydrates, even though reducing total calories, still keeps the insulin levels in your blood too high. Thus, the sugar gets stored as fat, and the cycle continues. The only way to burn fat is to reduce carbohydrates enough so that the fat-burning hormone glucagon gets activated.

Exercise, as valuable as it is, is performed to burn fat, because fat is the major storage form of energy in the body. But in order for this to happen, the body still needs to activate fat-burning hormones. It requires a tremendous amount of exercise to get to the point where fat burning for energy takes place. Low-carbohydrate nutrition tends to be faster and its weight-loss effects will last forever, as long as too many carbohydrates are not consumed.

Let's take a look at some of the popular foods Americans eat and see how much fat there really is in their diets. What do most people we know eat for breakfast? Certainly not the bacon and egg breakfast that we recommend. Bagels, juice, muffins, fruit, pancakes, doughnuts, coffee, and cereal with low-fat milk are what most Americans eat for breakfast today. Sound familiar? Perhaps some oatmeal, but most likely the instant type that is essentially sugar with a few oats. If your breakfast is made up of the above food items, then it is nearly 100 percent carbohydrates.

What about lunch? The classic American brown-bag lunch that most of us grew up eating, and unfortunately many of us still do, is a sandwich, potato chips, a piece of fruit, and a dessert. There probably is a can of soda added to this. Perhaps the sandwich is baloney and cheese, or a deli-meat sandwich, but it could also be peanut butter and jelly. In any event, this all-American lunch is again mostly carbohydrates. Potato chips have a large amount of carbohydrates along with polyunsaturated fats. But if you look at the whole lunch, you will see that it is mostly carbohydrates and virtually no saturated fat.

Dinner is probably the meal where most people actually eat a fair amount of protein and fat. There is often a protein dish, a vegetable, and a starch. This may be accompanied by a dessert. Usually there is some bread or a roll, and there's a chance that some people still spread it with real butter. Water and milk (often low fat) may also be served, especially to children. The amount of carbohydrates in this typical American dinner is probably still greater than 50 percent of the total calories, especially if the vegetables are corn or peas, which are very high in carbohydrates.

Many of us eat out at lunch and dinner, either at sit-down restaurants or something more fast-food oriented. Over and over it's said that eating at a fast-food hamburger joint is bad because there's so much saturated fat in such food. But is it really that fatty? A typical meal would be a hamburger with french fries and a soda. The burger has at most two thin meat patties that constitute the entire amount of saturated fat, but don't forget there is a large amount of bread in that bun! The fries and soda are mostly carbohydrates, except for polyunsaturated fats in the fries from the cooking oil. It's probably true that partially hydrogenated trans fats are unhealthy, but these are derived from vegetable oils and processed before they get into foods. In no way can these fats be lumped together with true saturated animal fats, which are in fact very healthy fats.

Obviously, we don't know what all of you are eating, but we've seen enough throughout the years to get a feel for what is consumed daily by many Americans. We've also talked to people who still believe that U.S. carbohydrate consumption is not that great, and that fat intake constitutes the majority of the average person's food intake. We suggest that you evaluate your own daily food intake to see how much carbohydrate you actually eat each day. We'll discuss more details of our nutritional program in chapter 12.

A LOOK AT THE NUMBERS

The United States Department of Agriculture (USDA) and the Centers for Disease Control (CDC) publish vast quantities of information about diseases and trends and about the average American diet. The information is obtained from periodic surveys and from death records and hospital and medical records. We scoured through much of the published information in the USDA "Continuing Survey of Food Intakes by Individuals, 1994–1996," and this is what was found. The numbers cited are for both men and women, averaged together starting from the age of five to about seventy years old.

First, let's take a look at the average daily intake of grain products that are consumed. Men over the age of twenty consume about 350 grams of grain products per day, and women over twenty consume about 250 grams of grain products per day. These numbers also were broken down into different categories. Cereals and pasta constituted about 80 grams per day; breads and rolls made up about 70 grams per day; snack foods, such as cakes, cookies, pastries, chips, pretzels, and so on, totaled between 100 to 150 grams per day.

These numbers go far beyond what the body needs for optimal health. We have shown that *only 72 grams or less of utilizable carbohydrates per day* are required to normalize insulin and reduce the risk of many diseases. Based on the grain numbers shown above, many adults are consuming more than four times that amount.

We've all heard the argument that it's the saturated fat within these products that are causing the problem. However, since these products are disproportionately carbohydrate, this argument is not convincing. Moreover, most of the fat in processed grain-based foods is unsaturated fat. Look at the food labels to see for yourself. The amount of nutrients these foods supply also is negligible. Chapter 9 provides some insight into the availability of vitamins, minerals, and other nutrients in various foods.

Let's look at some more numbers to get a clear picture of the average American diet. Saturated fat has been heralded as the primary cause of heart disease, cancer, diabetes, and obesity in this country. How much saturated fat does the average American eat each day? The same USDA survey shows that Americans got about 11 percent of total calories from saturated fat. Protein consumption each day was about 15 percent of calories. Carbohydrates made up 55 to 60 percent, and the rest was from unsaturated fats.

The numbers just don't add up. Saturated fat is supposed to cause all these problems with our health, yet only 11 percent of total calories are from this supposed culprit! Our research shows that, on the contrary, it is the carbohydrates that contribute to disease.

The story with beef consumption is also very interesting. Contrary to what is published in daily news articles and various health publications, beef consumption is at a rather low level. The average individual consumes about 30 grams of beef per day. This number represents about 0.06 pounds. Think of it like this: A ¼-pound hamburger patty contains 114 grams of beef. It seems apparent from this information that beef is not eaten every day. If we multiply 30 grams per day by seven days, we get 210 grams of beef, on average, consumed per week. This is about ½-pound of beef a week, which can hardly be seen as an excessive amount.

Now, compare this with the consumption of grain products. If 300 grams were consumed per day on average between men and women, that would correspond to 2,100 grams per week. *This equals 4.6 pounds of grains a week.* Wow!

So which are we eating too much of: meat at ½-pound per week, or grain products at 4.6 pounds per week?

We should also consider fruit consumption. Fruit has been given the green light in nutritional arenas: "Eat as much fruit as you want; it's good for you." Fruits and vegetables are believed to promote good health and eliminate many diseases, even though we have not seen enough good clinical scientific evidence to support this.

All foods should be judged by their health and nutritional assessment. Some fruits, such as oranges, bananas, grapes, and all dried fruits, are quite high in carbohydrates, whereas many vegetables, such as leafy greens and celery, are low-carbohydrate foods. Potatoes contain the most carbohydrate in the vegetable family, with corn and peas close behind. Between 1994 and 1996, the USDA survey showed that the average American consumed about 165 grams of fruit per day, with 65 grams coming from juice. Even the most "natural" fruit juice is simply sugar water with some vitamins thrown in.

A startling aspect of fruit consumption is that children under the age of five consumed more than 250 grams of fruit and fruit juice *per day*. This means that young children essentially are getting large amounts of sugar on a daily basis. Studies have shown that the growth of children who consume too much juice is either stunted or the children become overweight. It is vital that children eat fat and protein so that their musculature, bones, and organs are able to grow and develop normally. Children often experience myriad intestinal problems if they consume these excessive amounts of fruit and juice. Whole milk—not 2 percent or low fat—would be a much healthier beverage for all children.

Now let's compare the amounts of beef, grain, and fruit eaten by Americans in the survey. As stated earlier, the total amount of beef eaten a week averaged about a ½-pound per person; grains made up about 4.6 pounds; fruit weighed in at about 2.7 pounds. The amount of utilizable carbohydrate from grain products is around 80 percent, and for fruit (fruit juice is much higher), about 20 percent. Adding these together, we come up with a total of about 4.2 pounds of usable carbohydrates for grains and fruits combined. This means 4.2 pounds of glucose is consumed, which the body has to metabolize each week. If these foods are eaten throughout the day, then this could surely cause an insulin resistance problem in many people. Half a pound of red meat contains around 20 percent fat. Thus, 1/10 of a pound of saturated fat from beef is consumed, on average, in the American diet per week. It seems clear that carbohydrates are the problem, not meat consumption or its associated fat. Besides all the statistics, we have already shown you proof that lower carbohydrate equals better health.

Of course, these numbers are only approximations, and they also are averages. We could reasonably expect beef consumption to be greater in some people (and certainly less in others, especially vegetarians), and this caveat also applies to carbohydrate consumption. Still, these numbers are from the USDA.

OVERWEIGHT CHILDREN

A low-carbohydrate diet has essentially a defattening effect. The fact that carbohydrates are the basic cause of human overweight can be clearly seen in cases of juvenile obesity. Dr. Mackarness stated in his book *Eat Fat and Grow Slim* that children and adolescents afflicted with overweight could be treated successfully by reducing their carbohydrate intake. Children are the same as adults as far as diet is concerned, and all human beings are by nature meat and fat eaters. Primitive humans offered children the same foods they ate themselves, apart from mother's milk. For this reason, a low-carbohydrate diet is best for children, too. Children may in fact benefit even more, since at that point of development, hormones and growth are very active, and the foundation of proper eating habits is established. Doting parents who do not have the will to withdraw carbohydrates from their children's diets, are, in the long run, creating a lifetime health and addiction problem.

In Dr. Lutz's practice, a low-carbohydrate diet was always successful in children's weight loss. Weight loss in adults was more variable—that is, many were successful, but not all. In treating more than 100 extremely overweight adolescents, not one case ended in failure.[8] In patients who appeared not to respond, it was always discovered that the diet had either not been strictly followed or had been given up too soon. Apart from very extreme cases, a normal, slender figure was achieved within a year.

Of course, the scale is not the only criterion of success for children. Although the majority of fat juveniles lose some pounds at the beginning, increased body growth eventually adds pounds as the children convert their fat into length, muscle, skin, and bones.

One such case is shown in Figure 8.1. This thirteen-year-old boy weighed over 250 pounds when his parents brought him to Dr.

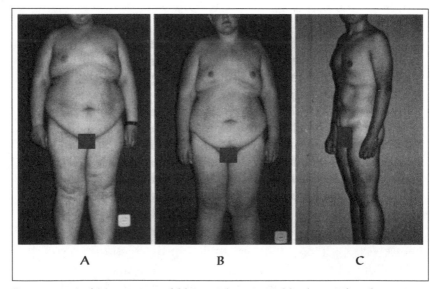

A   **B**   **C**

Figure 8.1 A thirteen-year-old boy with an initial body weight of over 250 pounds (*A*). After three months on a low-carbohydrate diet, marked reduction in body volume is already evident, and puberty begins (*B*). After two and a half years, the young man's figure is completely normal (*C*).

Lutz. Photo A shows the boy at his first visit. After three months, a marked reduction in body volume is observed in photo B. Photo C is the same boy after two and a half years on a low-carbohydrate diet. The change in his body is dramatic.

This boy is an example of an extreme case that required many years to fully recover from excess carbohydrate consumption. In this and similar cases, the excess weight from our carbohydrate consumption also delayed puberty: Once a low-carbohydrate diet was adopted, puberty took its natural course. The sex hormones in adolescents are increased when insulin is decreased because the decrease in the anabolic side from lower insulin production allows the body to produce sex hormones (other anabolic hormones) in sufficient quantities, as nature intended. Observations such as these indicate just how much a low-carbohydrate diet promotes the proper hormonal balance.

FAT ADULTS, STARVATION CURES

Now let's consider the obese adult. It is well documented that obesity is a risk factor for heart attacks and strokes, and that the tendency of obese persons to suffer from hypertension and diabetes further reduces their life expectancy.

It has become apparent in the course of more than forty years of experience with the low-carbohydrate diet that only some overweight adults attain an ideal figure within a reasonable period of time; men with a middle paunch and slender extremities usually fare best.

Feminine (pear-shaped) and masculine (apple-shaped) types of obesity can be observed in both sexes. The feminine type is fat below the waist, with broad hips, fat legs, and a girdle of fat around the abdomen. The masculine type is fat above, with a large and protuberant belly but relatively slender hips and extremities. The more pear-shaped an individual, the more difficult it is to lose weight, and in women, unfortunately, the approach of menopause makes it even harder. It is an invariable rule that the further the fat extends beyond the abdomen and hips to the extremities and to fingers and toes, the greater the difficulties in combating it by dietary measures. Some women even gain weight at the beginning of the diet, although usually only a little.

It would be dishonest to claim that everyone can attain his or her ideal weight on a low-carbohydrate diet. We also freely admit that we do not as yet know why one overweight individual responds to carbohydrate restriction when another does not. The only way to find out if you can lose weight and keep it off permanently is by trying the low-carbohydrate program. It seems that the best way to help people is to get them to adopt a low-carbohydrate nutritional program at an early age, thus eliminating the difficulties that arise in changing one's physiology after puberty.

The diet should in any case be given a chance before resorting to a fat-free, calorie-counting cure for obesity. Any form of calorie reduction should be made primarily at the expense of carbohydrates, not fat or protein. There are important reasons for this, as we shall discuss later. A low-carbohydrate diet will still benefit overall health, even if a desired weight is not achieved.

CARBOHYDRATE ADDICTION

Personal experience has taught most of us that carbohydrates, for reasons not fully understood, are addictive. Candy and sweets are always singled out, but all carbohydrates essentially offer the body what it is addicted to. It's very easy to eat too many carbohydrates because, somehow, there's a breakdown in the feedback mechanisms that are supposed to tell us when we're full. It's much more difficult to overindulge with fat and protein. Fat tends to create a more full feeling in the stomach. Perhaps the body is simply saying, "The carbohydrates you're eating aren't satisfying me!" so the eating continues.

FEWER CARBOHYDRATES OR FEWER CALORIES?

From what's been said so far, it's obvious that the same slimming effect cannot be expected from a low-carbohydrate diet with unlimited calorie intake, and a low-carbohydrate diet that involves a reduction in calories. Remember that ultimately we should all be concerned with overall health. Weight alone is not the only or even the best marker for health status. A muscular athlete will probably weigh more than an overweight individual because muscle has a higher density compared to fat.

In the case of a low-carbohydrate diet with no restriction of calories other than carbohydrate calories, a person loses weight but does not become thin, since weight loss takes place at the expense of fat tissue, and musculature and other organs profit. In the case of a complete restriction of calories, it is possible to attain any weight desired, and the result can be the lean figure of the Hollywood starlet or that of a model—chic for the purposes of exhibiting trendy clothes but useless for sport and other activities. Obviously, the low-carbohydrate individuals with their well-nourished organs are healthier than the clotheshorses who have sacrificed their protein reserves for an ultra-slim body.

HELP FOR THE THIN

There is a tendency for Americans and the popular media to focus solely on overweight people when body types are discussed. But there are people who are too thin, and for whom weight gain is crucial for their health. This is especially true for those approaching old age, when bone density becomes increasingly important.

The very thin carbohydrate eater usually has very little muscle with a very slight bone structure. These people tend to burn the excess energy from the overeating of carbohydrates, instead of storing it into adipose tissue as is the case in the obese/overweight body type.

On the surface, this burning of energy would seem a good thing, and very thin people often have an enhanced energy profile. This is only true, however, if a constant supply of carbohydrates is available. The thin carbohydrate eater cannot afford to even delay a meal. Metabolically, they are probably not too different than the over-weight carbohydrate eater. Thin people will also often experience low blood sugar episodes because they are still faced with the fundamental problem associated with eating too many carbohydrates: insulin resistance and hyperinsulinemia.

There is no available fat metabolism to provide the thin carbohydrate eater with a balance of energy. Thus, carbohydrates constitute the only source of energy for them. As with overweight high-carbohydrate eaters, fat metabolism is restricted. Because fat supplies the majority of energy reserves in humans, the thin carbohydrate eater must continually eat in order to satisfy the body's energy requirements.

The low-carbohydrate program augments the anabolic processes that contribute to increased body mass in the form of bone density, muscle, and connective tissue. But the underweight person must be diligent. It takes some time to begin to see the benefit of weight gain. Usually thin people experience a loss of weight during the first few months on the diet. This eventually gives way to increased body mass as the production of growth hormone eventually increases, and the nutrients needed to build tissue (fat and protein) are consumed. Over a long period of time, from one to two years, they will eventually reach a larger body mass compared to when they began the low-carbohydrate program. The new weight, however, will be in all the right places.

An example of the profound effects on carbohydrate restriction on the thin can be seen from the two photographs shown in Figure 8.2. These photographs were sent to Dr. Lutz from a man who had read of his work in Austria. The pictures speak for themselves, but below is the letter that accompanied these photographs:

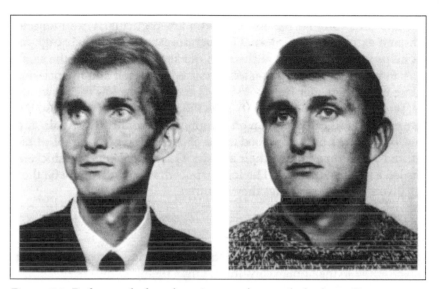

Figure 8.2 Before and after changing to a low-carbohydrate diet.

Two years ago, the book *Leben ohne Brot* by Dr. Wolfgang Lutz of Salzburg came into my hands. I read it with great interest and have followed its advice with success.

I am twenty-eight years of age, a student, and unmarried. The wrong type of nutrition—sometimes almost vegetarian, with vegetables, salads, little meat and fat over a longer period of time—was responsible for my weight of 44 kilograms, although I am 177 centimeters tall. My physical efficiency sank, my teeth were in poor condition, and my eyes weak. In my opinion, only the fact that I had been running regularly for years (even when weighing only 40 kilograms) and exercising a lot, accounted for the absence of more serious consequences. However, after an attack of weakness in my legs whilst on a long walk I decided to try a change of diet. Although I had already considerably cut down on carbohydrates, I now adhered strictly to Dr. Lutz's diet and included fat meat, sausage, and cooked liver (which I consider to be of greater value than other meat); two to three egg yolks occasionally; steamed, low-carbohydrate vegetables; about ⅛ liter of cream and 150 to 200 grams of butter daily; cheese; milk; a little uncooked fruit; and a small amount of curds. I gained 20 kilograms in three months. At my present weight of 60 kilograms I feel strong and am able to run as before. The changeover to a very high-fat diet was easy and there were no ill effects. Like Lutz, I am convinced that starchy food in large quantities is bad for us, and I would like to offer him my personal thanks for his book.

G. Z.

The dramatic change in the individual shown in Figure 8.2 represents yet another powerful piece of evidence that low-carbohydrate nutrition is the proper nutrition for all of us, whether young or old, big or small, male or female. Low-fat diets can never achieve positive, optimal growth at any stage of life.

We hope you fully appreciate the fact that overall health is what is ultimately important, and not just your weight. If you have a lot of muscle, for example, you will tend to weigh more because muscle weighs more than fat. You may have a large bone structure that adds to your weight. Americans need to shift their focus from a person's weight to a person's overall health.

While it's true that obesity is a sign that a person's health is somewhat compromised, the goal should still be an increase in overall health. Weight reduction is one way you can measure your successful change to better health, but it's not the only marker.

If you wish to change your current shape, we can confidently say that only by adopting a low-carbohydrate diet can you permanently attain your long-term goals. You will not have to starve yourself, but you will need to strictly adhere to the diet we describe in chapters 1 and 12. Remember: It's *not* your weight that's most important, but *how you look and how you feel.* We encourage you to begin now. You'll be glad you did!

CHAPTER NINE

Vitamins, Minerals, and Cofactors: The Myths Revealed

Up TO NOW WE HAVE FOCUSED ON various diseases that are blamed on excessive fat consumption. We've presented powerful evidence that the low-fat theory of nutrition has not fulfilled its promise, and that low-carbohydrate nutrition is a valuable tool in the fight against disease. This alternative to the fat theory is based not only on clinical information from over ten thousand patients in Dr. Lutz's practice, but also on basic biochemical facts and large amounts of published research data from many scientists and medical researchers throughout the world. We have presented a theory of nutrition that, while still not complete, explains many physical problems that people encounter today. The fat theory deals only with heart disease, and not very convincingly, as many researchers and medical scientists have found.

In this chapter, we will focus on vitamins, minerals, and cofactors. We'll define these terms a little later, but it's important to first debunk a popular myth: You *must* eat large quantities of fruits and vegetables to get your daily supply of vitamins. This is absolutely not true! While we do get some vitamins from fruits and vegetables, we can get most of them from animal foods.

Even more importantly, there are many vitamins and cofactors that we *only* get from animal foods. This means that if you don't eat any animal foods, you will probably develop a deficiency in some vitamins. You can, of course, take vitamin supplements to augment these deficiencies, but this method is not as good for your body as a combination of foods from an animal source. Don't misunderstand: We're certainly not suggesting you eliminate fruits and vegetables from your diet, *just that you don't consume more than 72 grams (6 BUs) of carbohydrates daily in all forms.* If, for you, this means eating less fruit, then we urge you to take this step. Your health certainly will benefit.

VITAMINS

Vitamins are small molecules that the body cannot make, so they must be obtained from the food supply. They are called small molecules because most molecules in the body are quite large, such as proteins, lipids, and nucleic acids, that is DNA (deoxyribonucleic acid). Another class of small molecules, vitamin-like substances called cofactors, will be discussed later in this chapter.

Vitamins perform a variety of functions. Many of them are needed to make enzymes (the proteins that speed up biochemical reactions) work properly. We mentioned a few vitamins that are part of enzymes in chapter 6. Dr. Kilmer McCully's discovery that deficiencies in vitamins B_6 or B_{12} or folic acid can give rise to high homocysteine levels is one example of the importance of vitamins. These three vitamins are each a component of a different enzyme necessary to metabolize and remove homocysteine from the blood.

Vitamins are not required in large amounts. Scientists and nutritionists have determined to some extent how much of these dietary components should be consumed each day, but these numbers should be considered only as guidelines. The complete story regarding vitamins has yet to fully emerge.

Vitamins perform so many important functions that we cannot possibly talk about them all here. What we want to emphasize is where they are obtained in the diet, a few of their more interesting functions, and their availability in animal and other low-carbohydrate foods.

Vitamins are classified as either fat-soluble or water-soluble. This means that, depending on their chemical structure, they can either dissolve into water or are more available from fat sources. This is an important distinction. Fat and water do not blend when put together, which you've no doubt noticed in a simple oil and vinegar salad dressing. The same type of chemistry takes place throughout your body. Fats tend to associate with fats and also lipid-loving small molecules.

There are at least thirteen known vitamins. Table 9.1 summarizes the major known vitamins and shows their classification as either water soluble or fat soluble. In Table 9.2, we summarize some of the best food sources of these vitamins. The food sources were obtained from a table prepared by the American Institute for Cancer Research in Washington, D.C., and from *The Yearbook of Agriculture*.[1] They are useful as a guideline, but are probably incomplete.

Let's take a close look at these tables, particularly Table 9.2. Out of thirteen vitamins, only *one* is not available from animal foods, vitamin C. (To be precise, there is a very small amount of vitamin C in animal foods, but probably not a sufficient supply to meet our

---

Table 9.1 Water-Soluble and Fat-Soluble Vitamins

Water-Soluble Vitamins	*Fat-Soluble Vitamins*
Thiamin (B_1)	A
Riboflavin (B_2)	D
Pyridoxine (B_6)	K
Cobalamin (B_{12})	E
Nicotinic acid (niacin)	
Pantothenic acid	
Biotin	
Folic acid	
C	

Table 9.2 Best Food Sources for Vitamins

Vitamin	Best Sources
A (carotene)	Liver, eggs, yellow and green fruits and vegetables, milk and dairy products
B_1 (thiamin)	Wheat germ, yeast, liver, nuts, fish, poultry, beans, meat
B_2 (riboflavin)	Whole grains, green leafy vegetables, organ meats
B_6 (pyridoxine)	Fish, poultry, meats, liver, vegetables, whole grains, bananas
B_{12} (cobalamin)	Meats, liver, eggs, milk, fish, cheese
Biotin	Yeast, organ meats, legumes, eggs
Folic Acid	Green leafy vegetables, meats, citrus fruits, whole milk products, liver, grains
Niacin	Meat, poultry, fish, milk products, peanuts, brewer's yeast
Pantothenic Acid	Meats, whole grains, legumes
C	Citrus fruits, vegetables, tomatoes, potatoes
D	Fish liver oil, egg yolks, meats, fortified milk
E	Vegetable oils, green vegetables, organ meats, eggs, nuts
K	Meats, soybeans, fish, wheat germ, egg yolk, green leafy vegetables

physiological requirements.) Two vitamins are *only* found in animal foods: vitamins D and B_{12}. Vitamin B_{12} is also called *cobalamin* because it contains the metal atom cobalt. Pure vegetarians are highly susceptible to B_{12} deficiencies if they do not take supplements, and they need to take great care to ensure they get all the necessary vitamins one way or another.

We can also see that many animal foods supply a good variety of vitamins in one single source. Out of the thirteen vitamins, six are supplied in reasonable quantities in eggs alone. Thus, consumption of eggs daily would supply at least half the body's vitamin needs, along with important fats and protein. As we have already seen, eggs do not represent a hazard to your health. They are arguably the most nutritious food available and also among the least costly. Many vegetarians still eat eggs, and this is perhaps the single most important food for them because this would be the only food they eat that supplies vitamins B_{12} and D.

Five of the vitamins are found in appreciable quantities in vegetables, of which four are in green leafy vegetables. Green leafy vegetables supply minimal carbohydrate and are, therefore, low-carbohydrate foods. Even vitamin C is abundant in vegetables such as broccoli, which also is a low-carbohydrate food. Fruits, on the other hand, are rather high in carbohydrates, and it is not necessary to rely on them for your vitamin supply.

Whole grains also supply a fair amount of some vitamins. Four of the vitamins in Table 9.2 are supplied by whole grains or wheat germ. The problem with grains—particularly processed grain foods, and most of the grains sold in foods in the United States today are heavily processed—is that overconsumption leads to the insulin-resistance problem. The nutritive part, the outer germ and kernel, are usually stripped from the wheat berry before the food is made.

The fact that our government often pushes for added vitamins in different foods is a clear sign that the mainstream foods are vitamin deficient. For example, the U.S. Department of Agriculture has approved the addition of supplemental folic acid to grain products. But if meat, whole milk, and green vegetables are consumed daily, there is no need to add vitamins to our grain products. It's simple: Just eat less grain and more of the foods that already contain the folic acid.

It's a dangerous contradiction for our health officials to tout grain products as being such healthy foods, yet admit there is a lack of any appreciable nutritional substance to them. Low in vitamins, low in protein, low in fats—what you have left are complex sugars, which break down in the intestine to become simple sugars. That's all!

Nevertheless, the consumption of grains is not completely detrimental, as long as 72 grams (6 BUs) of *total* carbohydrates or less are consumed per day. The long-standing USDA recommendation, via the well-known Food Pyramid, that large amounts of breads and grains should be consumed daily, is not based on anything other than ignorance. By default, because fats were regarded as harmful, grains have filled the empty space left behind. *But nowhere have we found good experiments to prove that high amounts of grains are beneficial.* This advice is simply, and sadly, the propagation of errors—one person said it, and the next, and the next, and eventually it has come to be regarded as "the truth." We have yet to read or hear of any disease that was treated successfully with a high-grain diet.

MINERALS AND MICRONUTRIENTS

Minerals also are very important for health, and are required for the proper function of a wide range of systems in the body. Certain compounds related to minerals are called *micronutrients*, or trace elements, because they are only required in tiny amounts, relative to the macronutrients we have mentioned: carbohydrates, proteins, and fats.

Minerals are individual elements. The Periodic Table of the Elements (which some of you may recall from a science class) is a summary of all the elements that have been discovered in the universe, many of which are functional parts of biological systems. Minerals operate similarly to vitamins in that they are part of enzymes and also participate in many important metabolic functions. Table 9.3 lists important minerals and micronutrients along with their food sources.

Calcium is an example of a mineral that is needed in relatively large amounts. It is known to be important for strong bones and teeth, for proper muscle action and blood clotting, and as a heartbeat regulator. The richest food sources of calcium are milk and milk products.

Women in particular are urged to supplement their diets with calcium to help reduce the risk of osteoporosis (thinning of the bones due to loss of bone mass). Calcium is absorbed into the body with the help of vitamin D, which is primarily found in animal foods. Instead of recommending that people drink more whole milk, eat more cheese, and avoid grains, our health professionals prefer to prescribe calcium supplements. Wouldn't it be better to eat the foods that actually supply the nutrients our bodies need?

People who are lactose intolerant should choose milk products that contain no lactose, such as cheese and cottage cheese. Fermented milk products are often easy to tolerate because the lactose has been converted to lactic acid by bacteria. Whole-milk plain

Table 9.3 Best Food Sources for Minerals

Mineral	*Best Sources*
Calcium	Milk and dairy products, dark leafy greens
Chromium	Brewer's yeast, whole grain cereals, clams
Copper	Oysters, nuts, organ meats, legumes
Iodine	Seafood, iodized salt
Iron	Meats, fish, green leafy vegetables
Magnesium	Nuts, green vegetables, whole grains
Manganese	Nuts, whole grains, vegetables, fruit
Phosphorus	Fish, meat, poultry, eggs, whole grains
Potassium	Meats, vegetables, fruit
Selenium	Seafood, nuts, meats, whole grains
Zinc	Meats, liver, eggs, seafood, whole grains

yogurt is one such food. But watch out for low-fat flavored yogurts. These contain high amounts of sugar, and are almost like liquid candy, without the beneficial fat.

Calcium is also found in appreciable quantities in green vegetables, such as broccoli, kale, and spinach. However, it is important to remember that calcium is absorbed into the body better in the presence of vitamin D (which is not in these vegetables), and that even if calcium-rich foods are consumed, a body heavy on the catabolic side will have difficulty in using the calcium to maintain and build bones, teeth, and nails.

Figure 9.1 presents data from some of Dr. Lutz's patients who adopted a low-carbohydrate diet. As you can see, calcium levels began to rise after a month on the diet and then leveled off at three months. No supplements were needed to accomplish this. Therefore, we feel that a low-carbohydrate diet will also be beneficial in reducing the risk of osteoporosis. It is not just the supply of calcium and other nutrients that is important, but how the body uses them. With a low-

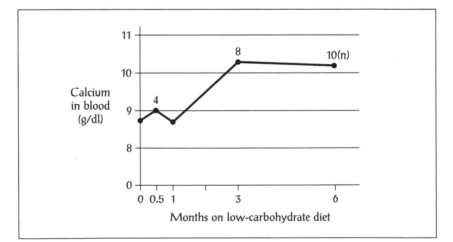

Figure 9.1 After one month on a low-carbohydrate diet, the levels of calcium in the blood begin to rise. They reach a plateau at three months. The number of patients measured at a given time is shown on the graph.

carbohydrate diet, the body produces more growth hormone and the breakdown of tissue is decreased. This means that bones will be maintained and not weakened from anabolic insulin overload. A low-carbohydrate diet will help to maintain strong bones and teeth.

Selenium is an example of an essential micronutrient. Although it is needed in trace amounts only, it is essential for our bodies. Selenium is a component of a special amino acid called *selenocysteine*. Selenocysteine was discovered by Thressa C. Stadtman at the National Institutes of Health. This discovery led to research worldwide that has proven selenium to be a critical component of at least ten mammalian enzymes.[2]

One of these enzymes is called *glutathione peroxidase*. The function of glutathione peroxidase is to eliminate the damage to lipid membranes and other molecules that have been destroyed from byproducts of normal oxygen metabolism. This is why selenium is called an *antioxidant*—because it is part of a macromolecular enzyme that performs antioxidant functions. Selenium is most abundant in organ meats, some nuts, seafood, and whole grains.

Another enzyme that contains selenium is called *thioredoxin reductase*.[3] This enzyme is critical for the formation of the body's DNA, which contains all the genetic information for cell division, protein synthesis, and ultimately reproduction.

From Table 9.3, we can evaluate the supply of all the minerals shown. Except for chromium, animal foods supply more of each mineral. Fruits supply only manganese. Five of the minerals can be found in grains, but it's been shown that the amount of the various minerals in grains, including selenium, is heavily dependent on the mineral supply of the soil in which they were grown.

Many published charts on vitamin and mineral supplies in foods are designed in a way that does not show animal foods to have large amounts of these vital nutrients. This is one way that people are led to believe that animal foods do not offer much in the way of these nutrients. Why is this done? Could it be in order to perpetuate the myths of low-fat, low-meat diets? The truth is, vitamins and minerals are abundantly available in animal foods, and generally animal foods supply more of them per individual serving than does any single serving of a fruit, vegetable, or grain.

One reason meats supply so many vitamins is because they are from animals that also need these vitamins to live. The similar physiology between some animals and humans is the reason animals do supply nutrients that closely match human needs. After all, people are much more closely related to a pig or cow than to a vegetable (well, most people, anyway!).

Another reason is that certain animals, known as ruminants (cattle, sheep, goats, buffalo, deer, antelopes), have bacteria in their stomachs that can make many essential vitamins and cofactors. Bacteria were the first organisms to inhabit the planet. They have the ability to make almost all the molecules from simple building blocks that they require for their existence. Higher life-forms lose the ability to make everything they need, so their food supply becomes more critical. In a symbiotic relationship, the bacteria that inhabit the stomachs, or rumen, in these animals will use the carbon-, nitrogen-, and oxygen-building blocks from grass, leaves, and some nuts to make vitamins and cofactors. The bacteria use these nutrients for their own metabolism, and they, in turn, are used by the ruminants. Thus, when we eat meats from these animals, we get a high-quality, balanced supply of vitamins. Not only are most of the vitamins and minerals essential for life found in abundance in animal foods, some of these nutrients are found only in animal foods.

COFACTORS

Cofactors are another very important class of small molecules. These vitamin-like substances can be made in the body or obtained from the diet, whereas vitamins can be obtained only from the diet (or via diet supplementation).

Several cofactors are worth mentioning here because they perform extremely important functions, and because they are primarily found in animal foods.

L-Carnitine

L-carnitine is an amino acid required to transport medium- and long-chain fatty acids into the mitochondria. It's generally believed that fatty acid molecules greater than about ten carbon atoms in length require L-carnitine in order to travel into the mitochondria. This process requires the action of two enzymes. The first enzyme allows the L-carnitine molecule to be added to the fatty acid. Once this occurs, the L-carnitine–fatty acid molecule is more permeable to the mitochondrial membrane, and the second enzyme can move the molecule inside the mitochondria. The L-carnitine molecule is then removed and gets transported outside the mitochondria, where it helps another fatty acid molecule get in. This biochemical cycle allows fatty acids to be used by the mitochondria to make ATP: the primary energy source that drives all biochemical reactions.

L-carnitine made scientific headlines when researchers made observations on identical twins who both experienced painful muscle cramps since early childhood. The biochemical status of many of the enzymes for energy production were evaluated, and it was determined that a deficiency of carnitine was responsible for the problems the twins experienced. This has led to a general conclusion that poor fatty acid metabolism of long-chain fatty acids is often accompanied by a deficiency of L-carnitine.

Excess carbohydrate consumption reduces the body's ability to metabolize fatty acids due to the anabolic effects of insulin. Because of this potential problem, our colleague Tom Nufert recommends that people beginning a low-carbohydrate diet consider taking an L-carnitine supplement for the first few weeks if they experience any muscle fatigue or cramping during that time. Table 9.4 shows the levels of carnitine in different foods.

In addition to its availability from dietary sources, the biosynthesis of L-carnitine also occurs in humans. This means that our bodies can make L-carnitine from other nutrients. In a series of metabolic reactions, L-carnitine is made from two amino acids: lysine and methionine. This process also requires niacin, vitamin B_6, vitamin C, and iron.[4] Although L-carnitine deficiency is an infrequent problem in a healthy, well-nourished population consuming adequate protein, many people appear to be somewhere on the continuum between mild deficiency and overt disease. It seems likely that the decreased anabolic (building) effect of excess insulin that accompanies high-carbohydrate eating would tend to reduce the biosynthesis of L-carnitine.

Scientific Studies

There are many studies on the effects of L-carnitine supplementation on humans and animals. However, long-term supplementation is not required for those on a low-carbohydrate diet; meat supplies ample amounts of L-carnitine. Moreover, since the anabolic over-

Table 9.4 Levels of L-Carnitine in Various Foods

Food	L-Carnitine (mg/gram)
Mutton	12.9
Lamb	4.8
Beef	3.8
Pork	1.9
Poultry	0.6
Pears	0.17
Rice	0.11
Asparagus	0.08
Margarine	0.07
Bread	0.05
Potatoes	0.00
Carrots	0.00

load effects of insulin are reduced, biosynthesis of L-carnitine is probably increased at the same time.

Still, it's worthwhile to look at the results of some scientific studies to show how important proper fat metabolism is to our mitochondria and our overall health. Most of the research is focused on heart disease and heart muscle function. This is not surprising because the heart primarily uses fatty acids derived from the diet for the energy necessary to keep it beating. The heart muscle contains the greatest proportion of mitochondria per cell in our body; up to 50 percent of the volume of a heart muscle cell is taken up by mitochondria.

Contrary to the typical view that low-fat diets promote a healthy heart, this type of diet can actually lead to *poor* heart performance, especially if the cells cannot carry out their functions due to lack of energy. A good review of the different studies of L-carnitine and heart disease is available.[5]

In one study, patients who were suspected of having acute myocardial infarction were either placed on 2 grams of L-carnitine per day or a placebo for twenty-eight days.[6] At the end of the study, many heart disease parameters were lower in the L-carnitine group. Measurements included electrocardiogram results, cardiac enzyme levels, left ventricular enlargement, and total number of arrhythmias. All these measurements were significantly improved in the L-carnitine group. In addition, the levels of lactate dehydrogenase were lower in the L-carnitine group after just one week of supplementation. Lactate dehydrogenase is the enzyme that intercepts pyruvate and reduces it to lactate before it can move into the mitochondria. This is the way that bacteria and our cells produce energy in the absence of oxygen. Lower amounts of this enzyme means mitochondria are functioning better through aerobic metabolism.

Some very interesting recently published data indicate that L-carnitine may also play a role in Type 2 diabetes and insulin resistance. In one study, the effects of L-carnitine on glucose uptake in cells was evaluated in both healthy and Type 2 diabetic patients.[7] Intravenous glucose with or without L-carnitine was given to the patients, and then their various sugar metabolism levels were evaluated. The researchers found that the L-carnitine group had an increase in glucose uptake but a decrease in plasma lactate concentrations. This suggests that glucose use by the mitochondria actually improved. The conclusion was that L-carnitine appears to improve insulin sensitivity in insulin-resistant diabetic patients.

Remember that L-carnitine deficiencies like these would not exist if enough animal foods that contain L-carnitine were consumed.

Coenzyme Q-10

Coenzyme Q-10 (CoQ10), also called *ubiquinone*, is a small molecule whose primary function is to promote respiration in the mitochondria through electron transport. CoQ10 is another important cofactor that can either be made in the body or obtained from food. The best food sources for CoQ10 are animal foods, because CoQ10 is fat-soluble.

Several important points need to be made before we look at some CoQ10 studies. As the well-known cardiologist Dr. Stephen Sinatra has reported, drugs that reduce cholesterol also interfere with the biosynthesis of CoQ10. This is because the biochemical pathway for CoQ10 synthesis is a branch of the same pathway where cholesterol is made. Since CoQ10 is required for the heart to produce energy, incomplete synthesis of this cofactor can result in reduced heart function. To make matters worse, heart patients are usually instructed to eat fewer animal foods in an effort to reduce cholesterol levels. This, then, is a double-whammy: no CoQ10 being made in the body and no CoQ10 coming from the diet—a recipe for disaster.

Sinatra also pointed out that an increase in cancer rates has been observed in those taking cholesterol-lowering drugs.[8] The relationship is all too clear: When the function of the mitochondria is disrupted, cancerous cells are more likely to emerge.

There are many studies that show the benefit of taking supplemental CoQ10 for heart disease and cancer, as well as neuroprotective effects in Parkinson's disease.

The simple message of this chapter is that, contrary to popular opinion, fruits and vegetables are not required for vitamins and minerals. In fact, essential vitamins and minerals reside in animal foods; moreover, many invaluable nutrients can only be found in appreciable quantities in animal foods. So the next time you're eating a piece of fruit or a serving of vegetables, ask yourself, "Have I had enough CoQ10, L-carnitine, vitamin D, selenium, calcium, and vitamin B_{12} today?"

After all, as we mentioned in chapter 2, Stefansson and Anderson admitted themselves into the Bellevue Hospital in New York and ate only meat for a year straight! And what happened to them? They left the hospital healthier than when they arrived!

CHAPTER TEN

Cancer: Another Disease of Sugar Metabolism?

CANCER IS PERHAPS THE LEAST understood and most feared degenerative disease to afflict the human race. There have been many scientific and medical observations that have brought about a better understanding of what cancer is and how it may develop, but still there is no general consensus on an exact definition of cancer. Often, cancer is described as cells that multiply uncontrollably. This is a reasonable definition, but it leaves out a lot of available information.

As has been the case with most aspects of science in the last century, the study of cancer has been selectively narrowed down to a series of what have been termed "reductionist approaches." This means that, because of the development of better tools, science has been able to probe the inner workings of the cell to evaluate very specific relationships between cancer and cellular changes. While this direction was inevitable, and certainly necessary, the reductionist approach also can lead a scientist down the wrong path because an observation at the molecular level does not always lead to a correct conclusion at the whole organism level.

We believe that this reductionist approach has hindered the development of a unified theory of cancer. In a classic paper published in 1953, James Watson and Francis Crick[1] established the physical nature of the gene. This discovery has led to a huge amount of research into human genetics and the DNA molecule. As a result, many diseases, including cancer, are studied mostly at the level of DNA. Even with the unprecedented outburst of research in the past thirty years, fewer than 5 percent of diseases have been directly linked to heredity and DNA. It's true that this area of research is really still in its infancy, but even when it is fully mature, the more difficult, and more important, task of looking at the organism as a whole will still be necessary to cure modern-day diseases.

Let's take a closer look at this stuff called DNA. DNA stands for deoxyribonucleic acid. This molecule exists both in the nucleus and mitochondria of cells, but mostly in the nucleus. The DNA molecule contains genetic information that duplicates each time a cell divides, which is how the genetic information gets passed to offspring. DNA molecules carry many genes, really just small segments of DNA, that contain the blueprint of each individual's genetic information.

Genes are the pieces of DNA that contain the blueprint for a specific protein molecule. It is this protein molecule that actually performs a specific task within the body, so when we discuss genetics and DNA, we're really talking about the biosynthesis of proteins.

A huge task lies ahead for medical research, for, when all the human DNA is discovered by the researchers involved with the Human Genome Project, they still will not know much about the actual proteins that each gene produces, about how the protein production is regulated, and how it fits in with the rest of the tissue and organs. In the hierarchy of life, the proteins combine to make cells, which combine to make tissue, which combine to make organs, and finally this all comes together to make the entire organism.

What this means is that, at some point, science and medicine will need to embrace some higher-order view of disease. We don't want to imply that we have all the answers, but we do want to stress that there is a consistent relationship between insulin resistance and many of our modern, age-related diseases, including cancer.

Even more important, a cellular-level explanation of cancer has existed since the 1950s, but has been virtually ignored since the discovery of the DNA molecule. In 1956, Otto Warburg published a seminal paper in the journal *Science* with the title, "On the origin of cancer cells." In this paper, he describes some of the known aspects of cancer cells.[2] The most important observation that he and others had made was that the production of energy in cancer cells is different than the production of energy in noncancer cells.

When we discussed energy production in chapter 5, we pointed out that energy production in eukaryotic cells (the higher life-forms, including humans) takes place primarily in the cellular organelles called the mitochondria. Prokaryotic cells, which are primitive cells such as bacteria, produce energy mainly by the oxidation of easily oxidizable substances, usually sugars. These two types of energy production are pivotal aspects of cancer cell growth.

In the rest of this chapter, we want to take a closer look at cancer cells, with a focus on energy production and the whole cell. We'll include some of Dr. Lutz's observations from his practice, and some recent studies about cancer and nutrition.

As with every other disease we've discussed, there are many myths surrounding cancer and nutrition. One of the most misleading is that high-fat diets promote cancer. This is just not true—in fact, many recent studies prove this. Once again, this is a case of the overlap phenomenon: You heard it from one person who read it in a magazine or from a story on TV that popularized the findings of a study that found only what its researchers wanted to find.

This chapter is our attempt to explain the link between cancer and carbohydrates. As such, we offer numerous hypotheses to relate to what has been observed in laboratory experiments, as well as in clinical observations. Direct long-term evidence is very difficult to obtain because of the nature of this disease.

DIFFERENTIATION AND CELLULAR EVOLUTION

Cell cultures are the cells in a colony of bacteria (or human cells) that are grown in a laboratory environment. Even though each cell acts as an individual life-form, they are all the same. The food supply in these cell cultures is used up by the bacteria until no more food is available, if it is not replenished. The bacteria do not work together as a whole—they just divide and eat.

Now, go back in time, to the very beginning of life on Earth. As global conditions began to change, life evolved. Individual cells began to emerge that were different from one another. The worm, for example, developed a primitive digestive system, and the cells in this digestive system are different than the cells in the worm's nervous system. This process of development continued for millions of years and eventually produced many new life-forms. This exciting process of becoming a specific cell is called *differentiation*.

The first cells that form after an organism's inception are not yet differentiated. This means that they can go on and become almost any type of cell. At some point, the cells do differentiate to become one specific type of cell. For example, in humans we have many different types of cells: liver cells, heart muscle cells, skin cells, and so on. Differentiated cells work together. They no longer divide and consume food at the expense of the others but work together as part of the system they represent.

The researcher Albert Szent-Györgyi explained that cells also have the ability to revert back to a cell that multiplies rapidly. His example was the healing of a skin wound. The necessity to replace large amounts of cells requires the organism to rapidly make the necessary cells. In this instance, the cells must multiply "out of control" until the wound is healed, at which time they must again slow down and work together.

It was M. Abercrombie who showed that two pieces of tissue placed a short distance apart in a tissue culture (a laboratory environment that supplies nutrients) would grow rapidly until they contacted one another.[3] As soon as this happened, the cells would cease to grow rapidly. Abercrombie described this return to slow cell growth as "contact inhibition." Cancer cells, however, do not have this contact inhibition; they continue to multiply uncontrolled, even after they contact one another.

THE PRIMITIVE CELL MODEL OF CANCER

Cancer cells form by changing so that they no longer represent the specific tissue or type of cell of their original differentiation. This process is called *dedifferentiation*, and the cells are considered undifferentiated cells. Early in the 1950s this proposed model of cancer could be summarized by the following statement:

> *Cancer cells are cells that have reverted to more primitive cells that behave less like eukaryotic cells and more like prokaryotic cells.*

This theory of cancer was promoted before the discovery of DNA. We feel that it's still the best explanation of cancer today because it fits best with all the available evidence, particularly evidence from whole cell studies. There are certainly changes in the genetic makeup of cancer cells compared to normal cells, but these are not necessarily the cause of cancer. They could also be a consequence of cancer. In any event, the definition above does not preclude that damage to DNA causes cancer but simply states that anything that sufficiently disrupts human cell metabolism can cause the cell to revert to a primitive state. In the next sections we will explore how carbohydrates can disrupt cell metabolism.

ENERGY PRODUCTION AND CANCER CELLS

It has been proven that cancer cells use fermentation to produce energy more than noncancer cells do. An excellent, but very scientific, review of the subject of energy production in cancer cells was written by Peter Pederson.[4] Fermentation is the process of producing ATP anaerobically, meaning in the absence of oxygen. ATP is the energy molecule that sustains all life. This is one piece of evidence that supports the primitive cell theory of cancer, as fermentation is a primitive form of energy production that began with the bacteria.

Human cells rely on this process only in extremely low oxygen conditions, such as strenuous exercise; usually our cells produce energy aerobically in the process called *respiration*. An important consequence of this variation in energy production is that fermentation requires easily oxidized substances as fuel sources. Sugars, some amino acids, and small fatty acids are easily oxidized, whereas saturated large-chain fatty acids are not.

Cancer cells actually make less mitochondria than the corresponding "normal" cell. This is why fat may actually decrease cancer, because adequate supplies of fat may ensure that mitochondria are "happy" and the cell will see no reason to change its course.

There also are various levels of fermentation and respiration in cancer cells. The slow-growing cancer cells produce the least amount of energy by fermentation, and the rapidly growing dense tumor cells produce the most energy by fermentation. Thus, the degree of reversion to a primitive form of energy utilization is related to how quickly the cancer cells multiply. Cancer cells also produce ATP from respiration. Often the more there is of fermentation, the less there is of respiration.

The observation that cancer cells have various degrees of fermentation has been confirmed by many studies. One such study looked at the effects of glucose on two types of cancer cells. Researchers used "cell lines" to examine the effects of various energy sources on mitochondrial respiration. A human cell line is some type of cell that has been removed from a person and is conditioned to grow outside the body in an incubator. Most of these cell lines are cancer cells, since this is precisely what is required to allow the cells to multiply indefinitely with a renewable fuel supply. Some of the cells can be isolated before they become fully cancerous, and can grow in an incubator for a while, but they eventually die out even if adequate nutrients are available. Only if they dedifferentiate can they be "immortalized" to live essentially forever.

In a study by researchers at the Institut de Physiologie in Toulouse, France, the mitochondria of colon cancer cells were analyzed for their ability to produce energy by respiration.[5] In this work, the cells were isolated either as differentiated or undifferentiated cells. The results of the incubator studies showed that the undifferentiated, more primitive cells used less oxygen and increased anaerobic fermentation for their energy production. Even more important was that these same cells respired better in the absence of glucose in the incubation medium, suggesting that this may be a way to redifferentiate the cells. But when glucose is added back to the medium, the cells resumed making energy by the anaerobic fermentation of sugar, and the aerobic respiration process was again diminished. The other cells were not as affected by the presence of glucose, and still behaved more as they would in the organism. Respiration was still maximal in the cells that were least like cancer cells.

What all this implies is that carbohydrates in the diet may be responsible for causing cells to become cancerous. Next, let's consider a connection between high-carbohydrate consumption and cancer.

INSULIN—THE SIGNAL TO CHANGE?

You already know that insulin—the hormone that specifically responds to carbohydrates in the diet—sends out signals all over the body. Hormones are messengers. They signal cells that something has happened and send messages for cells to perform tasks. For example, after carbohydrates are consumed, the levels of sugar and glucose in the blood rise. The body responds by releasing insulin from the pancreas into the bloodstream. The insulin helps the glucose get transported into cells, or it helps convert glucose to triglycerides for storage in adipose tissue.

We have shown that hyperinsulinism is a condition that can be alleviated by a reduction in carbohydrate consumption. We also know that insulin-resistant individuals as well as diabetics tend to have too much glucose in their blood. The carbohydrate theory of cancer is simple:

*Too much insulin and glucose in the blood can cause cells to
dedifferentiate, just as they do in cell lines, and thus
can be a primary cause of dietary-related cancer.*

We've already revealed that cancer cells prefer glucose for their energy source. This may be one reason that cancer arises from dietary influences. When the glucose levels get too high, cells may revert back
to the old program of using glucose as the primary energy source. Dr.
Sergey Gorlotov, a microbiologist, pointed out that the amount of
ATP produced from anaerobic glucose metabolism is very low. He
surmised that cancer cells, under the influence of an overabundant
supply of nutrients, would use up much more glucose than a corresponding noncancer cell. Perhaps nutritionally induced cancer is simply a way to remove all of this glucose. If it is, then continued feeding
of carbohydrates to cancer patients would not be a wise choice.

CELL SIGNALS

Cell signals are quite complicated, and many researchers are working hard to determine just exactly how these messages are sent. We
do know that all cells have receptors. Receptors are usually proteins
that are attached to membranes on the cell surface. They don't
move around freely as other proteins do but remain attached to a
cell membrane. Before insulin can transport glucose into a cell, it
must first bind to a receptor. When it does, the receptor actually
turns into an enzyme, and it sends a signal by a process called *tyrosine phosphorylation.*

It turns out that a very similar process is involved with many proteins that arise from oncogenes, the genes that make proteins that
are involved with cancer cell formation. Many of these genes make
proteins involved in tyrosine phosphorylation, which is similar and
related to the signal from insulin. Since cancer cells lose their ability to respire, genes that promote fermentation are also known to
"turn on" in cancer cells. There are also genes that tend to stop cells

from proliferating and becoming cancerous. The p53 gene is one of the more well known of these genes. This gene is intimately related to mitochondrial function.

There's no question that this is a complicated situation. We look forward to the time when the respiration and dedifferentiation processes are studied in relation to carbohydrates in the diet. Perhaps then a true connection between genes that promote and inhibit cancer and the food people eat can be fully understood.

INSULIN AND GROWTH FACTORS

Other connections exist between insulin levels in the blood and cancer formation. Insulin is related to other hormones called *growth factors*, which in turn are responsible for many aspects of regulation, including tissue repair and cell division. Growth factors constitute a subset of the major hormones. There is increasing evidence that an imbalance of certain growth factors that are related to insulin can give rise to cancer formation.

One of the important growth factors is called *IGF-1*. This stands for "insulin-like growth factor." Research in laboratory animals has shown that IGF-1 plays a major role in the modulation of tumor progression. In one study, researchers observed that IGF-1 injections promoted the growth of bladder tumors, and that a low-calorie diet reduced the blood levels of IGF-1.[6] Increased levels of IGF-1 are also associated with prostate cancer and breast cancer.

This finding is related to the hormone insulin because it is also known that IGF-1 levels in people increase if high-carbohydrate diets are followed, even if total calories are reduced.[7] Thus, there is a direct connection with increases in insulin levels in the blood and increases in IGF-1 levels. As we have already shown, carbohydrates are the foods that increase insulin levels. So you can begin to see the connection: Eating too much carbohydrate results in too much insulin, which can result in too much IGF-1. These hormones can go on to signal cells to change and become cancerous.

Obese people who are insulin-resistant—meaning their insulin is not working properly—do not have a significant reduction of IGF-1 under calorie restriction. This suggests that the hormone-resistant phenomenon is more widespread. Growth hormone, which is often observed to be at low levels in insulin-resistant individuals, also appears to be part of a huge "hormone-resistant" cascade of events that begins with too much insulin.

As we have said before, the two-component theory of health begins with hormonal balance. Remember the hormonal teeter-totter we discussed in chapter 3? It was a way of showing that the body will always strive to balance anabolic and catabolic forces. When insulin levels are too high for too long, there must be a hormonal response to counteract the insulin. This may be how signals are delivered that can promote the growth of cancer cells.

Even thyroid hormones are associated with IGF-1 and, therefore, cancer. When the thyroid hormone T_3 is low, IGF-1 levels are also low.[8] Thyroid hormones are on the catabolic side of the hormonal teeter-totter. If insulin is high from excess carbohydrate consumption, levels of thyroid hormones in the body may increase to balance the two sides. Increases in T_3 are also associated with increases in IGF-1, and IGF-1 is associated with increased cancer formation.

So, there is a connection between insulin and cancer at the organism level. A low-carbohydrate diet has been shown to decrease the output of a hyperactive thyroid, thus the output of the thyroid hormones. This will also reduce the levels of IGF-1 and, perhaps, the risk of cancer.

BREAST CANCER

Breast cancer was the most prevalent cancer in Dr. Lutz's practice. A total of thirty-six women with varying degrees of breast cancer were treated by surgery and also placed on a low-carbohydrate diet if they were not already eating that way. To this day, thirty-five of the women have had no recurrence or metastasis of cancer. This means that there was no movement of cancer through the blood to other tissues, or, if the cancer did move, the body's conditions were not amenable to the formation of metastatic cancer. These women were not placed on any chemopreventive drugs or radiation treatments—just on a low-carbohydrate diet. One woman out of the thirty-six was found to have cancer in her lymph region immediately after surgery.

EPIDEMIOLOGY OF CANCER

Epidemiology is the use of large population groups to attempt to answer specific questions, and most of the information available today regarding cancer consists of epidemiological evidence. These data can be difficult to interpret but may still be useful.

Following one of the largest and most recent epidemiological studies, the Nurses Health Study, many scientific papers were published that looked at breast cancer and risk factors. One paper published in the British medical journal *The Lancet* discussed IGF-1 levels that were measured in these American nurses between 1989 and 1990.[9] The researchers found that increased levels of IGF-1 correlated to increased risk for breast cancer in premenopausal women under the age of fifty. In postmenopausal women, there was no risk associated with IGF-1 levels.

There have been many studies done, in animals and people, that indicate that fat content in the diet is not responsible for breast cancer or any other cancer. We know there's a tendency to blame dietary fat for just about everything that goes wrong, but that's just a lazy way out. Time after time, the studies show it just isn't true.

Another paper that came from the Nurses Health Study evaluated the diets of 88,795 women who were free of cancer in 1980, and then followed them for fourteen years.[10] A total of 2,956 (3.3 percent) of the women were diagnosed with breast cancer over this time. Women who consumed 30 to 35 percent of their energy from fat had a slightly lower risk of breast cancer compared to those who consumed 20 percent or less of their energy from fat. The risk reduction was small, but there was definitely no increase in risk by eating more fat. This means the higher carbohydrate group probably had a greater risk of breast cancer.

To further evaluate the situation, researchers looked at meat consumption and cooking methods in a group of 32,826 women in the same study.[11] There was no association found between those who consumed the most red meat (up to one serving per day) and breast cancer. Furthermore, the method of cooking was not associated with the risk or incidence of breast cancer, including barbecue methods that would tend to burn meat.[12]

Over the years, there's been much discussion about sex hormone levels in women and the relationship of these hormones to breast cancer risk. Increased sex hormones as a potential risk factor in postmenopausal women has been confirmed from the recent Nurses Health Study. An evaluation of 11,169 women who were not using hormone replacement therapy (HRT) revealed that elevated levels of estrogen and other sex hormones significantly increased the risk of breast cancer.[13]

What happens to estrogen levels in women who adopt a low-carbohydrate diet? This question is best answered by looking at the results published by Dr. Lutz and his colleague Dr. Iselstöger, a Viennese endocrinologist.[14] These results are shown in Figure 10.1.

In this figure, the levels of urinary estrogens are followed over time in women on a low-carbohydrate diet. You can clearly see that estrogen levels decreased almost immediately after the low-carbohydrate food regimen began. Urinary levels of hormones usually follow closely with blood levels. After the low-carbohydrate diet was stopped at twelve months, the levels of estrogen began to rise again. This shows how carbohydrates can dramatically affect hormones in a very short time and is consistent with everything we have presented so far regarding breast cancer.

COLON CANCER

Colon cancer is usually blamed on a high-fat, low-fiber Western diet. All too often, we are told that eating more fruits and vegetables will reduce colon cancer risk. Although this view is propagated by many, there is very little evidence to support it.

In the aforementioned Nurses Health Study, 88,757 women between the ages of thirty-four and fifty-nine were evaluated to determine if the consumption of fiber had any association with colon cancer.[15] During the sixteen-year period, 787 cases of colorectal cancer were documented. The conclusion from this study was that there is no evidence to link higher intake of fiber with a decreased risk of colon cancer. *There was no difference between high- and low-fiber groups and colon cancer risk.*

Epidemiological studies are important, but they still do not fully answer the questions they're intended to address—they can only

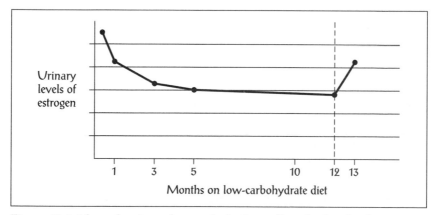

Figure 10.1 After adopting a low-carbohydrate diet, the levels of estrogen in the urine drop in women. After five months, the levels remain steady. At twelve months, the diet was stopped, and the levels of estrogen in the urine rose.

provide some suggestive correlations. We feel strongly that this needs to be understood for all the work that we cite in this book. We cannot deny that epidemiology has been the major source of information for those who promote the low-fat theory, and so we must also use the information if it disproves the low-fat theory.

A more controlled study on colon cancer was published in 1998. In this study, Australians were placed either on a low-fat, high-carbohydrate Chinese-type diet or on a typical Western (Australian) high-fat diet.[16] The researchers evaluated various fecal markers known to be associated with colon cancer. In all the markers they examined, the high-fat diet proved to be significantly better. These markers included fecal bulk, fecal transit time, fecal concentration of short-chain fatty acids, and levels of potentially damaging fecal ammonia.

The researchers concluded from the study that the consumption of a high-carbohydrate diet alone is insufficient to reduce the risk of developing colon cancer. Based on their results, one could also conclude that a Western diet may actually reduce the risk of colon cancer because many of the risk factors for colon cancer cited above were lowered for the high-fat diet group.

One important issue surrounding fiber in the diet is that true fiber is also a low-carbohydrate food. The problem with the fiber hypothesis is that most fiber comes with a large amount of carbohydrate. Fiber, by definition, is a nondigestible food substance. Foods that are promoted as high in fiber are often even higher in utilizable carbohydrate. You could eat a lot of bread, for instance, thinking you're getting a lot of fiber, when in fact you're getting very little true fiber but lots of very real carbohydrates.

One other important point about colon cancer and the diet concerns the benefits of fatty acids in the stool. Tom Nufert, a nutritional biochemist, has stated that one small-chain fatty acid, called *butyrate*, has been shown to differentiate cancer cells. This means it tends to reverse the process that we described previously about cancer, and makes cancer cells become normal. They become more like eukaryotes and less like bacterial cells. This may turn out to be very important in future colon cancer research. Butyrate is found mainly in butter.

SUMMARY

With all that is known about how cancer cells make their energy, about how cancer is formed, about the changes in DNA, and about the actual link between cancer and nutrition, it seems clear that we need to embrace the theories of yesterday to solve this problem today. Our bodies evolved to require mainly fat and protein. After all, we are humans and not bacteria. The message here is simple. Fat and protein are not the foods that cancer cells desire and need. We strongly believe that eating a low-carbohydrate diet reduces the risk of cancer because the most important food for cancer cells is glucose. The Eskimos who ate only fat and protein never had any cancer in their population until a Western (high-carbohydrate) diet was introduced. Why don't we ever hear of cancer of the heart? Probably because the heart uses almost all fat for energy, thus cancer does not have a chance to develop in those cells. We hope that researchers will take the next step and start looking at what has been known for a long time. Dietary related cancer is a sugar metabolism disease just like all the others.

CHAPTER ELEVEN

Evidence from Evolution: The True Fad Diet

TODAY IT SEEMS THAT THE ONLY medically accepted hypothesis about nutrition and disease is that fat is responsible for all that ails us. There is great pressure to conform to this theory, in spite of all the evidence to the contrary. Carbohydrates have been completely ignored as a potential problem in human diets.

However, as documented in the preceding chapters, the beneficial results of a low-carbohydrate diet, as observed by Dr. Lutz on thousands of people in his clinical practice, provide proof that is more than adequate. Loss of weight in obese adults and children; relief of the symptoms of endocrine disturbance; success in treating heart disease, hypertension, diabetes, and gastrointestinal diseases—all of these positive outcomes demonstrate the soundness of the low-carbohydrate hypothesis. One after another, the diseases of our civilization were shown to respond favorably to the low-carbohydrate diet, and the number of satisfied patients provided the reassurance that this route to health was indeed the correct path.

WHAT EVOLUTION TEACHES US

More than fifty years ago, Stefansson wrote that the inertia of the genetic makeup of higher animals (including humans) is such that the few thousand years during which the human race has practiced agriculture, and the couple of hundred that have elapsed since the

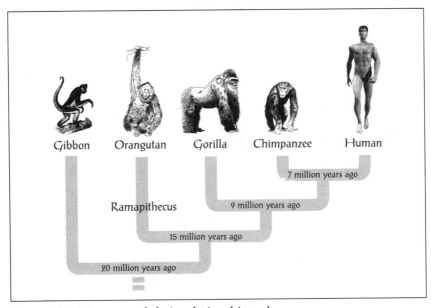

Figure 11.1 Primates and their relationship to humans.

discovery of refined sugar, are far too short a time for any noticeable positive evolutionary effects to have taken place. In other words, human physiology has not yet been able to adapt to this radical change in food. This concept has been a guiding light in the quest to unravel the true role of carbohydrates and fat in the human diet.

In a way, human beings are still the hunters, fishers, and gatherers that we were for hundreds of thousands of years before the ability to cultivate grain had been achieved. This is the principal argument from evolution: Humans have evolved and are adapted to eat a diet of mostly animal fat and protein. Too many people evaluate human health as if only the last twenty or thirty years count. Perhaps this is due to the mistaken notion that the present point in time is when the greatest human knowledge has been achieved.

People celebrate the fact that technology and medicine are on the brink of solving many modern problems, yet many diseases are increasing at a considerable rate. Whatever advances have been made, they cannot negate human physiology dating back millions of years. Ignoring the reality of the situation is counterproductive, but it's not too late to step back and take a realistic look at the available evidence. It's up to you, the reader, to take charge of your life, and to evaluate a low-carbohydrate diet to determine if it would be useful for you.

Approximately six million years separate us from our nearest primate ancestors, the chimpanzees. Agriculture began roughly 8,000 to 10,000 years ago. The time between agricultural development and today, compared to our evolution from hunters and gatherers, represents about 0.2 percent of the total evolutionary time. This tiny amount of time is insufficient for a species to successfully adapt to a major change in its food source.

Some people are so adamantly against the low-carbohydrate concept that they still insist that during evolution, humans consumed as much carbohydrates as are eaten today! This shows how illogical people can be when their sole purpose is to prove themselves right. There is just no basis for the often-heard argument that "people consume the same amount of carbohydrates today as before farming began." This is obviously not possible. After all, there were no grocery stores that sold cereals, breads, cookies, candy, pastries, bagels, potato chips, pretzels, and fruit juices during the Ice Age!

The structural alterations necessary for a large number of enzymes to adapt to metabolize large amounts of carbohydrates could require two hundred thousand to three hundred thousand years—each. Evidence for this has been found in two well-investigated proteins: the red blood pigment hemoglobin and the enzyme cytochrome C. In view of the millions of years that have elapsed since humans emerged from their apelike ancestral form to what we are today, a few thousand years make but a small difference.

Humans are constantly in the process of adaptation, but today we can all see what is actually occurring in this interim period when a significant environmental change is taking place, but physiology is not able to keep up with the change. Given the choice, do you want to be part of this experiment?

FROM CHIMPANZEES TO HUMANS

The fossil record is probably the purest form of evaluation into the ancestors of humans. Discoveries are being made constantly, and every five or ten years human genealogy is reassessed. What is known today is very exciting.

One of the most fascinating aspects of human evolution is that humans are the same single species throughout the world. Most of the other living organisms that inhabit the planet exist today as multiple species. For example, there are dozens of species of monkeys and hundreds of thousands of species of beetles. Antelopes, whales, and birds all have many species. But humans are only one: *Homo sapiens*. This in itself is an intriguing fact. Even our closest relatives, the great apes, fall into four species and many subspecies.

The fossil record has revealed that humans evolved in the same way as all other species, with numerous side-branches that ended up as dead ends. The simple picture that human evolution moved in a "straight line" is wrong: The evolution of a successful animal species involves many failures, and humans are no exception.

It is known for certain that humans descended from a common ancestor that developed in the course of some millions of years, with the gorilla on the one side and the chimpanzee on the other. The chimpanzees are our closest relatives in the order of primates. It is thought that the great apes and hominids (the first bipedal primates) split to a common ancestor between four million and six million years ago.

Nobody knows exactly how the transition from chimps to hominids took place. In 1974, the earliest known hominid was the famous "Lucy," a representative of the species *Australopithecus afarensis*, and she dates back approximately 3.2 million years. Older fossils have been discovered since that time—in 1994 and 1995, the oldest known hominid was discovered dating back about 4.4 million years. This species, *Ardipithecus ramidus*, is much closer to apes than to *Australopithecus afarensis*. Table 11.1 summarizes all the species that have been discovered after the split from chimpanzees, from fossils related to human evolution.

Table 11.1 A summary from the fossil record of the known species involved in human evolution, beyond the chimpanzees

Species	How Long Ago Species Lived	First Discovered
Ardipithecus ramidus	4.4 million years ago	Aramis, Ethiopia
Australopithecus anamensis	4.2 to 3.9 million years	Kanapoi, Kenya
Australopithecus afarensis	3.6 to 2.9 million years	Laetoli, Tanzania
Australopithecus africanus	3 to 2.3 million years	Taung, South Africa
Australopithecus aethiopicus	2.8 to 2.3 million years	Omo Basin, Ethiopia
Australopithecus garhi	2.5 million years	Bouri, Ethiopia
Australopithecus boisei	2.3 to 1.4 million years	Olduvai Gorge, Tanzania
Australopithecus robustus	1.9 to 1.5 million years	Kromadiaai, South Africa
Homo rudolfensis	2.4 to 1.8 million years	Koobi Fori, Kenya
Homo habilis	1.9 to 1.6 million years	Olduvai Gorge, Tanzania
Homo ergaster	1.7 to 1.5 million years	Koobi Fori, Kenya
Homo erectus	1.7 million to 250,000 years	Trinil, Indonedia
Homo antecessor	800,000 years	Gran Dolina, Spain
Homo neanderthalensis	200,000 to about 30,000 years	Neander Valley, Germany
Homo sapiens	about 200,000 years	

In the middle Awash region of Ethiopia where the oldest hominids were discovered (about 50 miles south of where Lucy was found), many more fossils have been retrieved. At the time of this writing, scientists are carefully evaluating these fossils. The idea that the "missing link" has never been discovered seems to be fading away, particularly since there will probably never be one specific link, as small changes in animals and fossils are observed over large periods of time. Even so, there is still no information on what evolutionary changes took place between about 4.5 million to 6 million years ago that eventually led to modern humans.

Our belief that humans evolved to be primarily fat and protein eaters is based on many factors, including evolution. It is a known fact that chimpanzees are fruit eaters, and this is sometimes used as an argument against humans being meat-eaters. However, this argument is unreliable. As we have already discussed, millions of years separate humans from the apes, and it is this period of time that needs to be addressed. Ample evidence exists that, at some stage, human ancestors were primarily hunters/scavengers of meat, whose diet consisted mainly of animal-derived foodstuffs.

But a pattern of meat eating already exists when we go even further back to the chimpanzees. The famous anthropologist Jane Goodall made the initial observations that apes are meat eaters. In a recent book by Craig B. Stanford, an associate professor of anthropology at the University of Southern California, the details of his observations of chimpanzees and other primates in the wild are presented. In fact, the title of the book speaks for itself: *The Hunting Apes: Meat Eating and the Origins of Human Behavior.*[1]

In this book, Stanford discusses the fact that chimpanzees do, in fact, hunt and eat meat. Their principle prey is the colobus monkeys. Stanford indicates that up to 15 percent of the chimpanzees' regular diet consists of freshly killed meat, mainly from small mammals. He also points out that meat is of particular importance in the chimpanzees' diet. Beyond just a food source, fresh meat is used as a tool of manipulation, and social interactions are required to produce successful hunts. Two other primates, the bonobo and orang-utan, also eat meat, but to a lesser extent than the chimps.

What this means is that meat eating among our ancestors clearly was already developed at the primate level; the idea that humans evolved from total vegetarians is simply incorrect. In reality, the gorilla, who is mostly vegetarian, is the "odd species out." But even gorillas eat insects, and that makes them slightly carnivorous.

Chimpanzees and gorillas differ by more than 2 percent of their DNA, but humans and chimpanzees differ by about 1.2 percent. This genetic profile, coupled with what is known about chimpanzees and gorillas, clearly indicates that the trend was toward more meat and fat in the diet even at the prehominid level.

EVOLUTION AND FOOD

The bones and teeth of the earliest known hominids (*Ardipithecus ramidus*) show a mix of chimpanzee-like and human traits, with smaller molars, larger canines, and thinner tooth enamel. Scientists interpret this as indicating they ate primarily a diet rich in easy-to-chew foods, such as fruits, nuts, leaves, and roots. It's reasonable to consider that there was only as much meat consumed as their closest relatives, the chimpanzees, had in their diet (15 percent), or perhaps a little more.

The introduction of stone tools is considered the beginning of the stage where human ancestors began to eat larger quantities of meat and fat. Tools specifically shaped from rocks have been found that date back more than 2.5 million years. At this time, our ancestors were upright-walking creatures, which freed up the upper body to use tools to hunt. This primitive beginning of technology allowed human ancestors to scavenge as well as hunt. According to many scientists, the creation of these implements caused a shift to high-energy, fat-containing animal foods. The discovery of fossils *from Australopithecus garhi* show that the animals were butchered and their bones and skulls cracked open, presumably for the nutritious high-fat bone marrow and brain.

These new high-energy foods are thought to have had all kinds of evolutionary consequences. One of these was the ability to explore a broader range of habitat, which eventually allowed the movement of our ancestors to other parts of the globe. Most importantly, it was also at this time that the fossil records indicate the expansion of the brain. Perhaps this was due to the availability of high-energy food, or perhaps the necessity to obtain high-energy food required an increase in brain size, but it is clear that this was a unique and defining moment in human history.

The transition to *Homo rudolfensis* and *Homo habilis* probably brought about the ability to catch small animals. The hunting of big game was a later development of *Homo erectus*, around 1.7 million to 500,000 years ago. The upright mode of locomotion, the liberation of the hands for other purposes, and larger brain development rapidly brought humans into the full possession of their mental capacities.

In addition, hominids scavenging in the volcanic Rift Valley may have had contact with fire. Signs of fire having been deliberately tended and exploited were later discovered in connection with Peking man, who lived about 350,000 years ago. The bones of Peking man, discovered just before the beginning of the Second World War in the Chou Kou Tien caves near Peking (now Beijing), were lost in the chaos of the fighting in China. Fortunately, casts and photographs of all the main finds were saved. Among these was a small stag horn, apparently carved with stone tools by some prehistoric person and hardened by fire. There were other indications that Peking man, whose brain was still at a relatively early stage of development, used fire for making weapons, preparing food, and as a source of light and warmth.

Treating raw food with fire is important for many reasons. Cooked meat can be consumed in a fraction of the time needed to devour it raw; bones become brittle when heated and the marrow more readily accessible. Cooked meat also does not spoil as rapidly as raw meat. This meant more time for hunting and, therefore, more high-energy food to eat.

THE ICE AGES

From about 1 million to 10,000 years ago, widespread glacial ice covered the Earth. This period is known as the Pleistocene epoch (the time more than 10,000 years ago that constituted the glacial age). Fire and clothing helped human ancestors survive the thousands and thousands of years taken up by the ice ages. By exploiting the vast quantities of game, human ancestors were able to spread throughout the entire Old World, right up to the edge of the glaciers.

About 150,000 to 30,000 years ago, squarely built creatures with apelike features, jutting eyebrows, and flat forehead—*Homo neanderthalensis*, otherwise known as Neanderthals—populated the entire Earth. This was in every respect a human being, with a brain weighing a little over 3 pounds. Stone implements found all over the world bear witness to the Neanderthals' manual skills. The variety of burial rites and the nature of the objects found in the graves indicate that they believed in the existence of supernatural beings. The dead were usually buried in a squatting position, bound up and sprinkled with ochre. This is the earliest known hint of metaphysical ideas.

For reasons that are not fully understood, the Neanderthals disappeared at the beginning of the fourth ice age, about thirty thousand years ago, and were replaced by modern *Homo sapiens*, more or less identical with present-day humans. There was an overlap of Neanderthal species with *Homo sapiens*, but eventually there was a complete convergence to modern-day humans. *Homo sapiens* were of a slender build with a high forehead. They possessed both technical and artistic skills, which were reflected in their success at hunting game, in their weapons and tools, and in the cave and rock drawings found over the entire earth. Naturalistic decorations and wonderful representations of game indicate the importance that was attached to animals as a source of food and clothing. Humans had even learned to form fine tools, such as needles, arrowheads and spear-tips, saws, and other domestic utensils from bones. About 10,000 B.C., at the end of the last Ice Age in Europe, the southern part of the continent was inhabited by an intelligent and technically skilled race of humans, prepared to follow the melting ice and to colonize the newly exposed land.

ENTER AGRICULTURE

In the 1970s, the distinguished anthropologist Marvin Harris published a wonderful book, *Cannibals and Kings*.[2] One chapter was devoted to a discussion of how and why humans made the transition to agriculture. Harris makes the argument that the practice of agriculture was adopted in various parts of the world after humans had severely overhunted the big game and small game could not supply all the food required for the ever-increasing population.

By 5,000 B.C., the connection between sowing and reaping had been grasped in the Nile Valley and in Mesopotamia (and perhaps even earlier in the Sahara, which at that time was fertile). Humans had learned to breed useful species of grain cereals by a process of artificial selection of grasses, and had also begun to domesticate animals. Settlements were established, and a class structure developed. Specialization into professions took place; laws were put into place; organized metaphysics, art, science, and politics followed. Cultivation of the land, irrigation, and animal husbandry—results of the Neolithic revolution—brought humans to the heights of social evolution within a few thousand years. But the costs of this evolution were high and the effects still remain today: The price was poor health for many.

This brings us to the main problem. Several adaptations to completely different forms of nutrition have been necessary since life first arose on this planet. In the beginning, during the abiotic-biotic transition, which stretched over about a billion years, nutrients consisted of carbohydrates. Later, animals lived on a mixed diet of plants and other animals. The first primates were insectivores, eating mostly animal matter (and some plant substances), whereas the apes succeeding them were mainly vegetarian, but also ate a fair amount of raw meat. As tree-dwellers, the apes' diet consisted chiefly of leaves, fruit, and shoots, some meat, but little starch.

Then, about six million years ago, the hominids branched off to develop along their own lines, and this involved a transition to the life of a hunter and to a diet consisting almost exclusively of meat and fat, which formed the bulk of the human diet until a few thousand years ago.

THE CARBOHYDRATE CURSE

When humans in Neolithic times learned to store the large quantities of starch harvested from fields for consumption all year round, it meant they no longer had to rely solely on hunting for their food. However, their metabolism was confronted with a difficult task. Up to that time, starch had only been available at certain times of the year, but never before in such vast quantities. It's conceivable that the constant intake of starch independent of any kind of annual rhythm must have led, via insulin, to overstimulation of the islet organ (readily seen in the sugar curves of fat children) where insulin is produced.

Scientific estimates of the percentage of calories obtained from cultivated plants during the early days of agriculture amounted to about 1 percent initially. That figure increased to more than 40 percent as agriculture became almost universal. This is the period when the human metabolism became corrupted by the rapid increase in carbohydrate in the diet, leading the way to the diseases of civilization. The technological innovations from agriculture and irrigation in some ways mirror what we see today. Unfortunately, innovation does not necessarily spell improvement in the health status of humans. Reduced exercise as a result of more automation and labor-saving devices comes to mind as a current dichotomy between progress and regress.

Evidence that carbohydrates contributed to poor health can be found from fossils obtained both before and after Paleolithic times. During the last thirty thousand years, skeletal remains have provided important clues. At the beginning of this preagricultural period, the anthropologist Lawrence Angel found that adult males averaged 5 feet, 11 inches in height and adult females about 5 feet, 6 inches. Twenty thousand years later, after agriculture and carbohydrate consumption were abundant, the males averaged 5 feet, 6 inches and the females averaged 5 feet.

Tooth loss at death shows a similar trend. In 30,000 B.C. adults died with 2.2 teeth missing; in 6,500 B.C. they averaged 3.5 missing; during Roman times there were 6.6 teeth missing.[3] These trends suggest that health was compromised by the introduction of large amounts of carbohydrates into the diet, and that the negative effects were experienced from the beginning.

Earlier we discussed Weston Price, a dentist who traveled the world in the 1920s and 1930s and found that groups of people who continually consumed milk, meat, and high-fat diets always have better bone structure and teeth, compared to their genetically equivalent relatives who adopted a high-carbohydrate diet. This also is observed in the fossil record.

The increase in population connected with the Neolithic revolution, mainly as a result of cultivation of the land, involved other disadvantages. Although mankind had always been afflicted by a wide variety of diseases, particularly those caused by bacteria and viruses, their spread had been limited by the isolation in which the individual groups of hunters lived. Living together with domestic animals probably challenged humans with new infectious diseases. The increasing populations of Neolithic times and the concentration into towns in Mesopotamia and in the valleys of the Nile and Indus must have resulted in epidemics.

The original and earliest inhabitants of such settlements probably had little immunity or inborn defense mechanisms to withstand the many diseases that now began to spread. Our forefathers must have experienced much the same fate as the Eskimos or the inhabitants of the Faroe Islands with the introduction of measles and tuberculosis, and the Europeans in the Middle Ages, with the importation of the influenza virus by Spaniards from South America.

IS ADAPTATION TO CARBOHYDRATES POSSIBLE?

With the new opportunities opened up by land cultivation and mass urbanization in the Neolithic age, humans embarked upon a path leading to the evolution of a new species. Thousands of steps involving mutation, new genetic combinations, and subsequent natural selection would be required to transform a meat eater into a carbohydrate eater. This process is not even complete today, as has already been discussed. Scientists are continually discovering more and more mutations in human genes that are associated with various diseases. Could some of these be due to too much carbohydrate in our diet? The answer is almost certainly yes.

Why haven't humans been able to adapt to this onslaught of high-carbohydrate nutrition?

During the ice ages, humans lived on a diet consisting exclusively of meat and other parts of the animal. The rigorous conditions of selection, which prevailed during glacial periods, must have led to complete adaptation of human metabolism to a diet of animal foods. Compared to the two million years of scavenging and hunting, and the thousands of years taken up by the ice ages, the 5,000 years (2,000 in Europe) that have elapsed since the introduction of land cultivation are much too short for the human organism to have adapted to a new type of nutrition.

If one looks at the incidence of disease related to migration of Europeans, a very interesting picture emerges. Societies that are closest to the Mediterranean region seem to suffer the least from the diseases of civilization.[4] This is the main region where farming began on this continent, which makes sense since this area would have been the warmest after the last ice age ended. When we look further north, more of our diseases afflict those populations. This is observed in available epidemiological data. Cancer,[5] heart disease, diabetes,[6] and multiple sclerosis[7] are more prevalent in populations who have been exposed to farming the shortest amount of time.

Populations that have been exposed to higher levels of carbohydrates for longer periods of time (10,000 years for example, compared to 2,000 years) have a genetic makeup that has had more time to adapt and, therefore, less disease is associated with higher intake of carbohydrates. Populations that have been exposed to carbohydrates the shortest amount of time seem to have minimal ability to deal with high-carbohydrate diets. This "adaptation theory" explains many observations about the diseases of civilization and the migration of population groups that began during the agricultural revolution and continues today.

The second reason why this adaptation is not yet complete can be found (as already stated) in the mechanism of evolution. Hunters lived in small clusters, which favored rapid hereditary changes within the group. In order to understand this, you must recall that every characteristic (gene) inherited from one parent corresponds to that same gene from the other parent. Most new or "abnormal" characteristics are recessive and remain undiscovered as long as they are dominated by a corresponding normal, dominant characteristic. Only if both parents contribute the same (new) characteristic does it become apparent in their offspring. This usually occurs if the parents are related, which is often the case in smaller sociological groups where intermarriage is more common. It has long been known that undesirable characteristics are passed on more readily in this way. We only have to call to mind the side-by-side occurrences of inherited diseases and highly undesirable characteristics so common throughout history. This is why intermarriage is frowned upon or forbidden in many cultures.

But the laws of inheritance also apply to the positive and normal characteristics that serve to improve a species. These come to light sooner in a small, inbreeding population where they can be perpetuated more rapidly by the process of selection. Thus evolution proceeded more quickly in the smaller social groups of primitive humans.

The transition from the Paleolithic period to the Neolithic with the invention of agriculture occurred in only 2,000 years in Europe (it took somewhat longer in the Near East)—certainly not a long enough period of time for the metabolism of early humans to adapt to the new style of nutrition.

In addition, grain cultivation made the existence of larger populations possible, thus slowing down the process of evolution seen in smaller groups. Newly inherited characteristics no longer came to light, as the probability of their being overshadowed by the existing characteristics grew with the size of the population and with the increasing possibilities of marrying outside the family. Selection and evolution were hindered in this way, including the natural adaptation of humans to this new type of nutrition. It can be said that the Neolithic revolution slowed down human evolution, and thus perpetuated the damaging effects of grain cultivation on human health.

Since today the drastic measures employed by nature in exterminating every ill-adapted individual cannot be imitated, nor can a return to smaller social groups be enforced, people will simply have to revert to eating primarily animal foods, or at least refrain from consuming excessive amounts of carbohydrate. Advances in the realms of biology, medicine, and agriculture will undoubtedly come to our aid, but the real path to progress in this case is to regress, at least with regard to dietary considerations.

Many sectors of our society benefit from the modern-day epidemic caused by carbohydrates; trillions of dollars are tied into society's continued push to eat carbohydrates—the processed food manufacturers, the medical practitioners, the insurance companies, the pharmaceutical companies—all have a strong financial interest in maintaining consumer ignorance about the relationship between nutrition, disease, and health. We are forced to believe that these people simply do not understand what is known, or perhaps choose to ignore the information. But surely the corporate heads of these companies, and their families, also suffer from many carbohydrate-related diseases!

We all look forward to the day when poor-quality, high in carbohydrate foods are replaced with high-protein and high–animal fat foods. It won't be easy. Society simply needs to be restructured, much as it was during the Industrial Revolution and the Information Age.

The first step is to accept that the low-fat theory of health is just plain wrong. As an individual, you can change your own life and regain control over your health and nutrition. You no longer need to have that candy bar or another helping of bread. Follow the low-carbohydrate nutritional program we outline in this book and you will undoubtedly experience better, healthier days ahead.

CHAPTER TWELVE

The Low-Carbohydrate Program in Practice: What You Need to Know

ONE OF THE ARGUMENTS AGAINST low-carbohydrate nutrition is that there is no knowledge of the long-term effects. In this book, we have presented the most comprehensive information ever published. We have detailed how low-carbohydrate nutrition can reverse many diseases that afflict our society. Based on the more than forty years that Dr. Lutz has used low-carbohydrate nutrition as a therapy to reverse many diseases, we are aware of the problems associated with the transition from high- to low-carbohydrate eating. In this chapter we will discuss these problems, along with the best way to approach the dietary change.

THE SOONER, THE BETTER

The sooner you begin to restrict carbohydrate intake, the better. A low-carbohydrate nutritional program can be adopted even in pregnancy because evidence now shows a benefit for both mother and fetus using low-carbohydrate nutrition.

Before reading further, please note these three important points:

1. The dramatic reduction of carbohydrates to almost zero levels promoted by various other authors is not necessary to achieve the health benefit of low-carbohydrate nutrition.

2. The 40-percent-carbohydrate diet promoted for athletes is not sufficiently low to achieve the health benefits demonstrated in this book.
3. Too rapid reduction of carbohydrates to almost none in the diet can cause serious initial side effects, if you are elderly or already have a major disease.

The level necessary to normalize insulin in the blood is about 72 grams of utilizable carbohydrates per day. This number is not guesswork—it's based on clinical results from measuring the blood glucose curves in patients who were insulin resistant.

However, the body's changeover to fat metabolism is only accomplished by reducing carbohydrates. How your body handles this change is dependent on your health status going into it. If you are already sick with some disease, if you are elderly, or if you have other health problems, a slow movement into the 72 grams per day regime is recommended. Even though a benefit may be seen by reducing carbohydrates to about 40 percent of the diet, as recommended by various authors, this amount is not sufficiently low to achieve the full benefit of low-carbohydrate nutrition.

INFANT NUTRITION

Mother's Milk

Human milk contains 1 to 2 percent protein, 4 percent fat, and 7 percent carbohydrate; cow's milk is 3.3 percent protein, 4 percent fat, and 5 percent carbohydrate. If no mother's milk is available for a child, an attempt should be made to adjust cow's milk (at least as far as protein, fat, and carbohydrate are concerned) to resemble human milk as closely as possible.

The old practice of diluting and sweetening cow's milk is not a healthy one. If the milk is adjusted to the correct protein and carbohydrate content by means of dilution and addition of sugar, its fat content is reduced to half or less of the original, which means that the milk is low in calories and the child is not satisfied. Instead of increasing the fat content, it is the carbohydrate content that is usually increased. But because infants dislike such a sweet mixture, starch in the form of rice water, semolina, or farina is often added instead of sugar.

There is no doubt that measures of this kind are unnatural. If rice, semolina, or flour were natural foods for a child, nature probably would have found a way to incorporate them into the mother's milk over the past millions of years. Increasing the carbohydrate content above 7 percent brings the milk to exactly the point that should be avoided at all costs; that is, an excessive quantity of carbohydrate in the baby's diet, leading to a later carbohydrate addiction and the chain of events that culminates in carbohydrate disease.

The following cow's milk formula has been used successfully to feed infants after breast-feeding stopped:

6 fluid ounces whole cow's milk
6 fluid ounces water
18 grams (4 level teaspoons) granulated sugar
30 milliliter (3 tablespoons) cream containing about 30 percent fat

This mixture can be boiled to be on the safe side, and is usually sufficient for two meals.

Fruit and Vitamins

Infants require nothing apart from the milk formula above. Fruit and vegetables, even in the form of juice, are unnecessary and only produce gas and abdominal cramps. An occasional drop of lemon juice suffices to cover their vitamin C requirements (heating the milk formula may damage its vitamin C).

After the twelfth month, an attempt can be made to increase the proportion of milk at the expense of water in the formula. After eighteen months, the general principles of low-carbohydrate nutrition can be applied. The carbohydrate levels should not exceed 15 percent of total calories consumed, with no more than one small piece of fruit per day.

Many of the problems experienced by mothers with their infants can be put down to faulty nutrition. Starch in any form—whether as rice water, flour, semolina, or similar foods—is completely unnatural for infants and leads to stomach pains. The baby screams, the family cannot sleep at night, and any attempt at routine is disrupted over and over.

The companies producing infant foodstuffs are well aware that they ought to simulate the natural composition of human milk and keep the carbohydrate below 7 percent in the final dilution. But parents often choose sweeter grain or fruit-based foods, the very foods that promote insulin overproduction and can lead to later carbohydrate disease. Next time you're in a grocery store, take a quick look at the ingredients in baby foods. You'll be surprised at just how high the level of carbohydrates is.

CHILDREN

It is a parent's duty to combat poor nutritional habits wherever possible, and this duty begins at the beginning of the child's life. The very foundation of carbohydrate disease—obesity, diabetes, hormonal disorders, and arteriosclerosis—are laid down *in utero*, or at least in early childhood. If care is taken that children are not given too much carbohydrate, they will be less endangered later in life.

All too often we hear that "carbohydrates are the only thing this child will eat." But no child is born with the desire to consume bread, sugared cereals, pastries, candy, fruit, and soft drinks. These treats are given to them, usually by doting parents, but these initial offerings begin a lifelong addiction that can cause many health problems. Sooner than you would think, children begin to crave only nonnutritious foods.

HOW MUCH IS ENOUGH?

The human pancreas contains a starch-splitting enzyme called *diastase*, which indicates that our bodies are prepared for certain amounts of carbohydrate—but what are these amounts?

If you recall the composition of mother's milk, with 7 percent carbohydrate as lactose, 1 to 2 percent protein, and about 4 percent fat, you see that carbohydrates account for about 40 percent of the total calories. However, it is important not to confuse lactose (milk sugar) with dextrose (sugar from starches), or a child's nutritional needs with an adult's needs. An adult requiring 2,500 calories daily who consumed the appropriate amount of mother's milk, would get 270 grams of carbohydrate (22.5 BUs), which would contribute 1,100 of these calories. But the composition of mother's milk is not relevant to adult nutrition. This food is custom-made for infants; its composition is suited to the energy requirements of the infant with its relatively unfavorable surface-to-weight ratio, and reflects the body temperature and needs of a time when warm-bloodedness was developing.

In the preinsulin era, the amount of pure carbohydrate empirically calculated as being permissible for a diabetic was 72 grams daily. An uncomplicated case of diabetes responds well to this treatment, and further restriction brings no additional advantage (except perhaps more rapid weight loss). Lower amounts of carbohydrates are usually not beneficial, probably because the body needs this amount of sugar from the diet, while the rest can be made directly from protein and fatty acids.

If you calculate the requirements of the brain, which has the greatest carbohydrate needs, and the requirements of the other organs, which need less, you will arrive at the number of 9.4 grams of carbohydrate needed per hour, which adds up to about 72 grams for the period of time needed to digest three meals (eight hours). This means only as much carbohydrate should be eaten as you are able to use during digestion itself. Anything more than this is a disadvantage, since it has to be converted into fat with the aid of insulin and leads to a state of hyperinsulinism, the main cause of today's diseases. Remember that any excess sugar that is not used must be stored in adipose tissue, and this requires energy. Perhaps this is why people who eat a high-carbohydrate meal often feel tired immediately after. Their body is fatigued because energy is needed to store the excess sugar. Those who eat a low-carbohydrate meal will not get tired immediately afterward.

These 70 to 80 grams of carbohydrate are a "prudent diet" in the truest sense, and represent a compromise between a normal high-carbohydrate way of eating and complete abstinence from carbohydrates. With low-carbohydrate nutrition, there is no need to go hungry and no stress reaction is observed.

WHAT TO EXPECT

A physician who intends to prescribe a low-carbohydrate diet, or a person who has decided to adopt such a diet, has to remember that the actual damage done by large amounts of carbohydrate cannot be reversed. There is a considerable difference between putting someone on a low-carbohydrate diet in his or her youth, and in converting the metabolism of people aged forty, sixty, or eighty.

No great damage will result from transplanting a sapling if it is moved with a large clump of the surrounding earth, but in order to transplant a fully grown tree, it is inevitable that some or many of its roots would be truncated. The larger tree will droop for some time, and it may not survive the upheaval at all.

The situation is rather similar when an adult or elderly person is put onto a low-carbohydrate nutritional program. Their metabolism is accustomed to large amounts of this type of food, and has in a way come to terms with this abnormal type of nutrition by developing certain regulatory measures (too much insulin, for example). The intestine, too, has grown used to sugar and starch. A changeover to a diet completely lacking in carbohydrates suddenly confronts the body with an entirely different situation. It now no longer needs the measures that had been necessary for utilizing the carbohydrates; instead, it has to learn to cope with more fat and protein.

The following sections will detail some of the experiences people had who adopted a low-carbohydrate nutritional program. These observations are based on thousands of patients over many years.

Loss of Appetite

Obese patients generally experience no negative consequences after changing to a low-carbohydrate nutritional program. They usually enjoy a good appetite and are pleased that they are losing weight in spite of eating plenty of food. Underweight persons as a rule at first lose about 3 to 6 pounds, but usually regain weight later. They often lose their appetite after a while, and develop an aversion to eating, particularly meat. It requires considerable powers of persuasion to keep them going; if they are going it alone, they should know that after their metabolism adjusts, they will experience a multitude of benefits. Remember that this change to a fat-burning and fat-utilizing metabolism by reducing carbohydrates is somewhat like eliminating an addictive drug. In the end, there will be great benefit, but the transition may be difficult.

In the case of some thin people, what remains from the carbohydrate days is not more appetite (as in the case of the obese), but less. The disappearance of hyperinsulinism on the low-carbohydrate diet removes one of the reasons why such patients ate at all—their hypoglycemia. Generally, thin individuals are driven to eat by low blood sugar, not by a general hunger.

It's important for these people to know beforehand that they may experience difficulties in the changeover, so that they don't have the impression they're the wrong types of people for low-carbohydrate nutrition. In fact, just the opposite is true, since thin people profit more than anyone from the diet. We have seen plenty of cases where extremely thin patients have been transformed into happy, sturdy figures with a normal weight.

It has been mentioned already that it's unwise to proceed too radically with this diet. A restriction to 5 to 6 BUs equal to 60 to 72 grams of pure carbohydrate, is ideal, and clears up gastrointestinal complaints (heartburn, bloating, diarrhea, colitis) most rapidly. Understandably, people are prepared to cooperate when they see an improvement. In the case of older people (over forty-five), some extra caution during the changeover is necessary.

Blood Clots

Animal fat that contains abundant saturated fatty acids has certain effects on the body's clotting system. This seems to be connected, on the one hand, with the heparin requirements (a protein that inhibits clotting of the blood) and, on the other, the formation of the clotting enzymes. The occurrence of thrombosis in occasional instances of a too-rapid changeover to a low-carbohydrate diet might be due to the state of starvation in which the body finds itself—expecting carbohydrates, for which it is prepared, it instead receives fat and protein, for which it is not immediately equipped, or not ready to handle in high quantity.

Thrombosis often occurs in stressful situations. For example, there is a tendency for thrombosis to occur following surgical procedures, childbirth, and severe physical exertion. Likewise, the changeover to the genetically correct diet of high fat and protein can be a stressful situation to the body. And the bigger the change, the greater the stress.

Those who are reducing their carbohydrate intake from, say, 40 percent down to 72 grams per day (10 to 20 percent of total calories) will experience fewer problems than those who have been consuming 80 percent of their daily calories as carbohydrates. The same holds true for age and existing health conditions. Thus, the people who eat the most carbohydrate often are the ones who have the most health problems, so they would naturally experience the most difficult transition, just as a person addicted to the highest dose of a drug will have the most difficulty in the early stages of reducing the drug.

Dr. Robert Atkins was accused of provoking heart attacks with his low-carbohydrate diet back in the early 1970s, and he was even invited to a hearing of the U.S. Senate because of it. In principle, Atkins's diet is the same as ours; however, his suggested procedure radically differs from the one used by us: Atkins initially withdrew all carbohydrates and relaxed the restriction afterward, whereas we never go below 6 BUs (72 grams of carbohydrates) out of caution, and hold the reins rather more loosely at the beginning. We don't know just how many heart attacks have been caused by the zero-calorie diets that became popular a few years ago. We do know that every sudden change in the body raises the blood-clotting tendency and can therefore elicit a clot at an already damaged place in the circulatory system, hence a catastrophe. Our low-carbohydrate program is by far the safest and most effective. We are confident in saying this because it is based on data from thousands of patients with diseases who have been treated by Dr. Lutz since the late 1950s.

One could exclude from dietary treatment those individuals whose age places them at increased risk for heart attacks (men over fifty and women over sixty), but that would not be doing them a favor, since they would be barred from a fundamental healing of their illness. Only a low-carbohydrate lifestyle is capable of putting a stop to arteriosclerosis and, therefore, to subsequent heart attacks.

People who are overweight with a sedentary lifestyle, who have diabetes, high blood pressure, or heart problems, should ease into carbohydrate restriction (e.g., beginning with 9 BUs) and only try to reach the desired 6 BUs over a few months. If you have any of these conditions, we urge you to be completely up front with your physician about your desire to begin a low-carbohydrate program. The intention should be that you work together to observe the results. Some intermediate medications may be necessary during the transition, such as blood-thinning agents like aspirin or coumarin. If you're taking cholesterol-lowering drugs, you will probably find that you're able to slowly reduce the amount taken as your health improves. These drugs are not particularly useful anyway, since low cholesterol is not a good marker for heart disease, and they suppress the levels of CoQ10.

Unfortunately, there are some people whose health is already compromised to the point of no return. If nothing is done, they have a heart attack; if something is done, the attack can occur through side effects of the low-carbohydrate treatment, as discussed above.

Bleeding Gums

After the transition to a low-carbohydrate diet, it is not unusual to see a swelling and bleeding of the gums for a short while. This could be due to excessive growth of certain tissues because of an increased level of growth hormone, or from inflammation as a result of increased immune responses to bacteria in the mouth.

If this happens to you, don't be too concerned. These symptoms will stop after a few months and never return. In fact, the gums and teeth benefit greatly from carbohydrate restriction. After the initial bleeding episodes, the gums will be strengthened. Your dentist will marvel at how little your gums bleed during cleaning, and if you're cavity-prone, the incidences of cavities will diminish as well. Of course, regular dental hygiene, including daily flossing and brushing, is always prudent. Very sick people should consult a physician if their gums bleed for more than a few weeks, but even then the low-carbohydrate program should not be given up.

Constipation

The large intestine can be expected to give some trouble. As has already been mentioned, the occurrence of constipation is typical in people who have previously suffered from it (less so in people with a normal stool before a low-carbohydrate diet is adopted). A diet containing large quantities of carbohydrate is harmful to the large intestine. This is because the fermentation of sugar and the large amount of ballast and roughage present stimulate emptying due to its cellulose content, and it favors bacterial growth. These people have only been spared chronic constipation because the carbohydrates acted as an ever-present laxative. In fact, under the influence of these carbohydrates, it is the pancreatic polypeptide hormones that speed up passage through the bowel that act as this laxative.

If carbohydrates are withdrawn, the emptying stimulus is lost and the constipation gradually becomes worse. It is vital that no compromise be made with respect to carbohydrate reduction. In the case of constipation, the most natural means to help the bowel through troubled times is a daily enema consisting of 1½ liters of warm water.

If this is too difficult, you can use one of the over-the-counter laxatives, or try an herbal laxative. Eventually, when its musculature has recovered and the hormonal regulation of bowel movement has reestablished its equilibrium, the constipated bowel regains its capacity for normal forward movement. Water should be consumed to eliminate thirst, but not to drown your insides.

Immune Reactions

A large part of the difficulty involved in readjusting the metabolism is due to stimulation of the immune system. If one considers how the quality of every tissue in the body improves, how thin people put on weight, skin becomes stronger, and the musculature, at least in weak individuals, is strengthened, it is no wonder that the immunocompetent cells share the benefits and produce more active substance than before low-carbohydrate nutrition is adopted.

This is a good thing. Colds, flu, and common infections are greatly reduced after a low-carbohydrate diet is adopted; wounds heal faster; women who were plagued with vaginal yeast infections usually see a marked reduction in these.

But stimulation of the immune system can also be a problem. It is possible that the immune system will mount an inadvertent attack on the body's own tissue. People who have an existing autoimmune disease should continue their currently prescribed therapy while they adopt the low-carbohydrate nutrition that we describe. The overall benefit to the tissues and organs on a low-carbohydrate diet will help most people, even those with autoimmune diseases. We know of a few people with autoimmune diseases who have had great success with the diet, but we do not have specific data from large population groups.

The Unconquerable Infection

Before both of us began a low-carbohydrate diet, we were ill fairly often with various conditions—one cold after another, or a cold following a bout of flu. Often a simple head cold would migrate into the lungs and bronchitis would develop. After adopting the program, all this changed. Now we hardly have any infections at all, or they are short-lived. However, some people experience a strange feeling, like they have a cold, but there is no infection and they don't necessarily feel ill. We have found that a simple treatment with 10 to 12 miligrams of cortisone or prednisone (these are steroids that inhibit the immune system) for four to five days is sufficient to eliminate the minor problem. You will need to consult with your physician for these treatments.

We call this feeling the "syndrome of the unconquerable infection." It may be due to the fact that, as the immune system strengthens, tissue that had even a slight infection gets rapidly and aggressively attacked by the immune system. Steroids will temporarily stop this process. As the tissue returns to normal and the initial infection disappears, no additional autoaggression will take place. This is merely speculation, but the clinical outcome of using a short steroid regimen has been shown to be very effective.

In people who live on a low-carbohydrate diet from childhood, no tissue damage develops; therefore, the syndrome of the unconquerable infection also cannot develop. But the opposite is true in a latecomer to the diet. This person's immune system is already programmed to a variety of infections, and the low-carbohydrate diet makes very powerful reactions possible—the immune system may deal most efficiently with an infection but then call with particular intensity for damage to tissue, which the body consequently is not able to avoid. Some people benefit from taking cortisone for a few days after almost every infection.

Asthma

The process described above is quite particularly applicable to people with bronchial asthma. Here we must distinguish between spastic bronchitis and genuine bronchial asthma. The first is purely degenerative; namely, breathing difficulties are brought about by loss of lung tissue, which is compensated for by a narrowing of the small branches of the bronchial tree. In these instances, a low-carbohydrate diet helps by stopping any further destruction of the lung tissue and improves the function of the lung tissue still available.

In contrast to this, caution is advised in genuine asthma. With its increased level of growth hormone, activation of the immune system by a low-carbohydrate diet can lead to a rapid increase in breathing difficulties and to circulatory problems. Therefore, again, first cortisone, then the diet, and perhaps cortisone again. This therapeutic scheme also applies to the other diseases of autoaggression (e.g., polyarthritis or lupus).

Heart and Liver

Very similar symptoms have been observed in cardiac patients. Atrial fibrillation occurred in three patients a few months after the changeover to low-carbohydrate nutrition. This again was thought

to be due to autoaggression by the immune system on the musculature of the heart.

Such tendencies will be awakened in most of the patients who
have an existing disease. Even so, the positive effect of the diet out-
weighs these autoaggressive experiences. In patients with heart disease, a slow decrease of carbohydrates, beginning with 8 to 10 BUs
per day, is the best approach.

The liver also is endangered by immune reactions. This large organ
harbors large numbers of white blood cells between its lobes, which
are responsible for setting off immune reactions. Thus, it is wise to an-
ticipate complications on a low-carbohydrate diet for people who have
existing liver disease. In practice, immune responses to the liver only
occurred in special and particularly severe cases of existing disease. If
you have a liver disease, your doctor can monitor the gamma globulins
to determine if any negative effects are observed using the diet. In
most patients suffering from chronic hepatitis, a gradual improvement, not to be achieved by other means, can be observed.

Rheumatism

The most common complaint of elderly people after changing to a
low-carbohydrate diet is that they are bothered by rheumatism for
some time. The attacks usually occur during or following a viral infection because an infection stimulates the production of immune
bodies (antibodies). It usually suffices to take a few milligrams of
prednisone tablets for several days in order to put an end to the
trouble. Again, consult with your doctor about these medications.

Vaccination

Vaccination is done in anticipation of infections. Clearly, today's
level of human health would not exist nor be kept up without im-
munization. The eradication of smallpox is undoubtedly a great

feat, which would not have been possible without the inoculation of the people of the world. In time, similar progress will surely be obtained with other diseases.

People who eat a diet low in carbohydrate have a much stronger immune system compared to before they reduced their carbohydrate intake. For these people, the inoculation becomes a superinoculation, and their reactions to it may be much stronger than expected. Frequently, there may be an overreaction by the immune system that has to be tamed with a steroid. Should this situation arise, consult your doctor to get a small dose of prednisone or cortisone.

In patients with ulcerative colitis, a relapse seen after a vaccination against ticks indicates a possible causal connection. Therefore, people with immune diseases should consider doing without vaccinations rather than run the risk of an abnormal immune reaction that could exacerbate the disease. With care, infections by others can be avoided. Safety measures should include frequent hand washing, no sharing of phones or office equipment, and avoiding crowds, especially during the cold and flu season. Being around children makes this much more difficult, of course.

WHEN THE LOW-CARBOHYDRATE DIET DOESN'T WORK

Experience with many thousands of patients on low-carbohydrate diet has convinced us that the body's immune reactions play a large role in human disease, and not only in connection with a low-carbohydrate diet. Much depends on how the illness itself develops, but above all, the immune reaction itself is the primary factor, and whether or not the immune system recognizes the carrier of the disease as such.

In high-carbohydrate eaters, perceptible immune reactions will only occur later because of poor tissue quality (including the immune system) and because of increased production of hormones from the adrenal cortex. But once the immune system has a "shot" at an organ, the transition to a low-carbohydrate diet will increase the organ's resistance to attacks by the immune system. The immune reactions of this improved immune system will be strengthened, too.

So, somewhere in the development of a disease there comes a point that precludes recovery; both opponents receive the same reinforcements and a stalemate prevails.

Still, there can be other causes for the irreversibility of a disease. High blood pressure frequently becomes fixed over the course of years. The explanation given is that, in the course of a long illness, changes occur to the blood vessels which then require or lead to higher arterial pressure because of circulatory disturbances to the inner organs, especially the kidneys.

Obesity is another example. It's easy to treat before puberty, but the older a person is, the sooner there are failures in treatment. Some obese adults, particularly women, don't lose any weight at all on a low-carbohydrate diet.

If Type 2 diabetics are treated at an early stage of the disease, the disease progression can actually be halted, but the older a person is and the longer they've been suffering from the disease, the smaller their chances are for a complete reversal. The same applies to elevated cholesterol and uric acid levels.

Even so, many elderly people who have an existing disease have benefited greatly from carbohydrate restriction. Even if there is not a reversal of symptoms, a healthier lifestyle and thus improved quality of life can be achieved. And after all, what's the alternative? To continue with a nutritional program that caused the metabolic disorder in the first place? That's not really an alternative.

In all probability, our bodies respond with well-meant regulatory mechanisms to the disease state initiated by excess carbohydrate. A case in point is the obese patient. Carbohydrates are the primary cause of this condition, and the body responds with an overproduction of insulin, which the adrenals counter in their turn by pouring out more sugar hormone (cortisone). If the cause is removed soon enough (i.e., if the carbohydrates are restricted) these effects can also be reversed.

But if consumption of more than 72 grams of carbohydrate is continued, the excessive production of insulin becomes a permanent state. With sexual maturity or in pregnancy, the countermechanisms are further enhanced by sexual hormones. Now the body has to think up something new, and this takes the form of insulin resistance. The cells become deaf to the calls of insulin and, under certain circumstances, diabetes develops. Apparently, the body has no other choice.

If restriction of carbohydrate in the diet at an advanced stage of a disease does not always bring the desired results, this should not be interpreted as meaning that the carbohydrates were not responsible for the disorder in the first place. It is quite simply, and sadly, that a point of no return has been reached.

HOW TO BEGIN

In healthy people under forty-five, the initial goal of 5 to 6 BUs daily can be aimed at as soon as you begin the program. This allows only small amounts of sugar and an occasional dessert, some crumbs for breaded food, a little lactose (in milk), and small quantities of carbohydrate in vegetables and fruit. Otherwise, the program consists entirely of animal food.

A very important point needs to be made here: *In the case of people older than forty-five or those with an existing heart condition or immune disease, begin with at least 9 BUs.* Great care needs to be taken so that this limit is not initially surpassed. This is a good precaution, and it will tend to ease the older or very sick person into a low-carbohydrate program without a potential "stress" condition of changing the diet too rapidly. Later, the carbohydrates consumed can be slowly reduced even further.

Fruits and Juices

Another important point: *It is a common mistake to underestimate the carbohydrate content of fruit and fruit juice.* One glass of orange juice (about 8 ounces) contains 20 to 30 grams of sugar (2 or 3 BUs). Large quantities of fruits and vegetables, even in the form of juice, are neither healthy nor well tolerated. Fruit juice is simply sugary water with a few vitamins thrown in. And when consumed, it's certainly better to eat the actual fruit itself, so the stomach at least has the potential to feel full before too much sugar is consumed.

The American habit of consuming large quantities of juice every day is ill-advised. It's been only a few thousand years since humans began to cultivate fruit trees, and squeezing fruit or vegetables to make juice is even more recent. The idea that raw fruit and vegetable juices are a particular aid to health arose several decades ago in connection with vitamin research, but that theory has now been discredited.

Many vegetables are relatively low-carbohydrate foods, but fruits definitely are not. The USDA Food Pyramid that advocates eating five to nine servings of fruits and vegetables a day is dangerously imprudent. We maintain that fruits and vegetables and their juices do not carry the same health benefits as fat and protein foods.

Alcohol

The metabolic breakdown of alcohol via acetaldehyde to acetic acid is rather similar to the breakdown of fatty acids. The extent to which alcohol has to be subtracted from the carbohydrate ration has yet to be decided experimentally. But in our experience, if sugar and starch are carefully watched, a little alcohol can be included with a clear conscience and without any harmful effects. One or two bottles of beer a day or a few glasses of wine won't do much harm. Hard liquor in moderation is also reasonable, but care should be taken not to consume drinks that are rich in sugars, either from the mix or the liquor itself. Straight liquor, or liquor combined with club soda or water, would probably be best, if that's the choice.

Preparation of Meat

It's usually better to make as few rules as possible, but to adhere to them strictly where the connections are obvious and results can be expected. Roasted or boiled meats are definitely not of equal value, as the appearance of the fat immediately shows. Boiled fat remains white whereas fried or roasted fat is transparent. This is due to changes in the fatty acids when they are heated in air. Despite these obvious differences, we don't wish to warn against roasting, or to advise boiling the food. After all, a roasting spit is a far older kitchen implement than are cooking pots. We can assume that we've already adapted by evolutionary means to these side effects of social development. Some researchers suggest that roasted meats can be carcinogenic from the burning of the food, but no reliable study has ever proven that to be true.

Fat

The only hope of keeping up a low-carbohydrate nutritional program and achieving the desired success is to replace the missing carbohydrates with fat. Humans cannot live on protein alone. In some Central American states, feeding political opponents only lean meat was an elegant way of getting rid of them without resorting to more violent measures. After a few months, diarrhea develops and death soon follows. Stefansson reported a similar chain of events in Canadian Eskimos who had to live on lean caribou meat for long periods of time without being able to catch fish.

It is now known that there are certain fatty acids required for human life; known as the essential fatty acids, these must be consumed in the diet. Although carbohydrate and fat are not equivalent, they can to a certain extent replace one another. Theoretically, this is understandable because carbohydrates are first turned into fat, and then the fat can be used for energy.

It would seem to be a logical and obvious measure for anyone eating less carbohydrate to make up for this by eating more fat. But in practice one comes up against the most surprising things. People willing to try a low-carbohydrate diet still want to consume a low-fat diet. Why? Fear of fat is the primary reason.

We have shown ample evidence throughout this book that it's carbohydrates that play the major role in disrupting the physiology so disease can occur. As long as your level of carbohydrates does not exceed 70 to 80 grams per day, then a high-fat diet is not only healthy but also necessary to achieve optimal health. Remember that the low-fat diet is based on erroneous observations perpetuated for generations and hammered into the consciousness of the general public by the media. If fat is not increased to compensate for reduced carbohydrate in the diet, people tend to satisfy their hunger with more plant and animal protein instead. Remember that gastritis, to offer just one example, cannot heal in the absence of fat.

All too often, people have memories of indigestion after a rich meal that contained a lot of fat. But you can be sure there also were plenty of carbohydrates, probably spices, and possibly even alcohol involved.

THE PRINCIPLE OF
LOW-CARBOHYDRATE NUTRITION REVISITED

To review, each 12 grams of carbohydrate is called a bread unit (BU). Six or fewer bread units are allowed per day, with unlimited quantities of any other foods. Adults over forty-five or those with an existing heart condition or immune disease should begin with 8 or 9 bread units per day. The table on pages 218–222 gives the carbohydrate content in BUs of a wide variety of familiar foods. There are many books available that offer similar information. Care needs to be taken to determine the amount of utilizable carbohydrate in various foods if they are not in the table. To dramatically reduce the risk of many diseases and also have the best chance of healing an existing condition, we recommend you consume about 72 grams of utilizable carbohydrates per day.

Unlimited amounts of animal foods can be eaten. You can enjoy eggs, cheese, creams, sour cream, meat, fish, pork, chicken, and animal fats. Butter can be eaten freely as this supplies the necessary fat needed to replace carbohydrates without large amounts of protein, and butter offers a plethora of vitamins and other essential nutrients. It is better to avoid polyunsaturated fats (particularly transfatty acids such as margarine) in large quantities. These fats are highly processed and are under increasing scrutiny as a potential negative dietary component.

Olive oil is the best of the vegetable oils. It contains 75 percent oleic acid (long-chain monounsaturated fat), 13 percent saturated fat, 10 percent linoleic, and 2 percent linolenic acids (the two essential fatty acids). However, olive oil should not be the only fat consumed. Butter, coconut oil, or palm kernel oil are important because they contain more short-chain fatty acids, which have many health benefits, such as faster energy utilization, antimicrobial properties, and anticancer properties. Also, too much olive oil may generate an imbalance of the essential fatty acids. Butter has much fewer essential fatty acids, but they are approximately in balance.

Watery fruits and vegetables like tomatoes and cucumbers, and to some extent watermelon, can be eaten in any quantity. A wary eye has to be kept on the carbohydrate content of all other plant foodstuffs. Sugar, with 12 grams of carbohydrate per BU, and flour, rice, semolina, oatmeal, and corn-based products, with their 15 grams of carbohydrate per bread unit, should be avoided.

Those people with gastrointestinal problems should completely avoid every kind of grain product containing gliadin, including wheat, rye, barley, and oats, at least until the condition shows a marked improvement.

A GOOD BREAKFAST

Breakfast is probably the most important meal of the day. Many people eat so much in the evenings when the day's work is done that they sleep badly and are unable to eat a good breakfast the next morning. This cycle must be changed. Eat a breakfast consisting of cheese and butter or several eggs with some type of meat. Even if you're unable to stomach it at first, a good breakfast should remain your goal. We've found that in time this will not only become easy but very enjoyable. A good meat and fat breakfast assures you of an amazing amount of energy for the entire day. You'll no longer be bound by weakness and hunger in the late morning. This allows for a whole different planning schedule at work and will surely increase your productivity. You'll be especially glad when twelve o'clock comes around and you're not so hungry that you feel weak. You will no longer have to wait in long lines because you can take your lunch later!

As far as the other meals are concerned, protein and fat should always be eaten first, as it's easier to turn down sweets and other dessert temptations if the edge has been taken off your appetite. If these guidelines are observed and your day begins with a good healthy meat or egg breakfast, instead of an empty breakfast of a bagel and a glass of juice, then you'll find it's easier to withstand carbohydrate temptations during the rest of the day.

RECIPES AND DINING OUT

There are recipes in nearly every cookbook that are perfectly suited for a low-carbohydrate diet. It's the choice of what to eat that plays the major role in planning meals. If you want a fish dish, use a fish recipe—just don't eat the rice or potato. Instead, replace that starch with a green vegetable (with lots of butter!) or a salad. A good cookbook that we recommend is *Nourishing Traditions* by Sally Fallon with Mary Enig, Ph.D.[1] This book not only offers many recipes of all kinds, but it contains a lot of nutritional wisdom.

Let's face it—nutritional programs that have specific daily meals are useless. Each of us leads a very different life, and individual (or family) eating habits vary greatly. In our program, just restrict your carbohydrates to 6 BUs. The rest is up to you.

Some plant foods contain very little carbohydrate—for example, leaf and stalk vegetables such as lettuce, spinach, asparagus, tomatoes, cucumbers, and mushrooms. Even root vegetables in moderate amounts are harmless. But you must always pay close attention to your consumption of grains as well as fruit and juice. These have rather high sugar contents, and this is often where underestimation occurs. Remember that fruit has never been shown to be healthy in excess by any study that looked directly at people with a disease. The common practice of lumping fruits and vegetables together is simply incorrect.

We hope that you now understand that low-carbohydrate nutrition is the healthy choice. We have given powerful evidence about the long-term effects of this type of nutrition. When people tell you this is a "fad" diet, ask to see their evidence that high-carbohydrate diets are healthy, and that diseases are successfully treated with their diet. We wish all of you a happy and healthy life.

Appendix:
Carbohydrate Table

The table on the following pages indicates the number of bread units (BUs) that different foods contain. The BUs were calculated from the percent of utilizable carbohydrate of each item. This table is meant to be a guide only. Not all foods are represented. Remember that there are 12 grams of utilizable carbohydrate in each bread unit. If a specific food is not shown on the table below, you can calculate the bread units of the food by dividing the total amount of carbohydrate shown on a food label by 12.

Total Carbohydrate ÷ 12 = Bread Units (BUs)

Foods that can be eaten in unlimited amounts are not shown in the table. These foods include beef, chicken, pork, fish, cheese, eggs, most other animal foods, and many vegetables (see the table for specific amounts in vegetables). Foods to limit are sugars, starches, and high-carbohydrate processed foods. Fruits need to be figured into the daily carbohydrate consumption because they generally contain a large amount of carbohydrate.

Frozen Foods	Serving Size	BUs
Healthy Choice Bowl Meal	9.5 oz.	2.5
Pizza	13 oz.	7.5
Fish sticks	6 sticks	1.5
Lasagna	1 slice	2.5
Corn dog	1 dog	2.0
Chicken, fried	3 oz. (1 piece)	0.5
Macaroni and cheese	1 cup	3.0
Waffles	2 waffles	2.5
Pancakes, blueberry	3 small	4.0
Tater Tot potatoes	10 tots	1.8
French fries	18 fries	1.5
Salisbury steak TV dinner	11 oz.	3.0
Turkey TV dinner	17 oz.	5.0
Blackeyed peas	½ cup	1.7

Breads		
English muffin	1	2.0
White	2 slices	2.0
Wheat	2 slices	2.0
Dark rye	2 slices	3.3
Hamburger bun	1	1.8
Bagel	1	3.7
Tortilla	1	1.7

Grains, Flour, Pasta		
Cereal, dry		
Raisin Bran	1 cup	5.0
Cheerios	1 cup	1.5
Frosted Flakes	1 cup	3.0
Flour, white	1 tablespoon	1.0
Flour, whole wheat	1 tablespoon	1.0
Oatmeal, raw	½ cup	2.3
Oatmeal, instant	1 packet	2.8
Rice, white	¼ cup	3.0
Rice, brown	¼ cup	2.7
Pasta, any kind	¾ cup	3.3

Snacks	Serving Size	BUs
Pretzel	5 pretzel (1 oz.)	1.8
Crackers, saltines	5 crackers	0.8
Cracker, Triscuits	7 crackers	1.8
Chips, Doritos	11 chips	1.4
Rice cake, peanut butter	1 cake	1.0
Protein bar	1 small bar (4 oz.)	1.0
Power Bar	1 bar (8 oz.)	5.4
Snack bars, all kinds	1 bar	2.3

Sugar & Sweets

Ice cream		
Breyer's Vanilla	½ cup	1.3
Ben & Jerry's Cherry Garcia	½ cup	2.2
Cookie, Oreo	2 cookies	1.6
Dark chocolate, 70% cocoa	4 squares	1.0
Pudding, pre-made	1 container	1.9
Sugar, white	1 tablespoon	1.0
Sugar, brown	1 tablespoon	1.0
Cupcake, chocolate	1	2.5
Doughnut, glazed	1	1.9
Cake	1 slice	2.9
Jelly, all fruit	¼ cup	2.3
Syrup, maple	¼ cup	4.4
Honey	1 teaspoon	1.0
Corn syrup	1 teaspoon	1.0
Molasses	1 teaspoon	1.0

Nuts

Walnuts	½ cup	0.8
Pecans	½ cup	0.7
Brazil	½ cup	0.7
Almonds	½ cup	0.8
Peanuts, in shell	½ cup	0.6
Peanut butter	2 tablespoons	1.2

Fruit	Serving Size	BUs
Grapefruit	½	0.8
Cantaloupe	½ (⅔ cup)	1.0
Orange	1 medium	1.5
Grapes	handful	1.5
Apple	1 medium	1.0
Applesauce	½ cup	2.0
Strawberries	⅔ cup	1.0
Banana	1 medium	2.0
Pear	1	1.3
Apricots, dried	¼ cup	2.5
Cranberries, dried	¼ cup	1.0
Prunes	5	2.4
Raisins	½ cup	2.8

Dressings & Sauces		
Chunky Blue Cheese	8 tablespoons, ½ cup	1.0
Fat-free Italian	8 tablespoons, ½ cup	2.5
Ketchup	8 tablespoons, ½ cup	3.5
Mustard	8 tablespoons, ½ cup	0.0
Mayonnaise	8 tablespoons, ½ cup	0.0
Spaghetti sauce, bottled	½ cup	0.8

Vegetables		
Beans, dry		
Pinto	¼ cup	2.0
Kidney	¼ cup	2.0
Mushrooms	1 cup	1.0
Asparagus	5 stalks	0.3
Broccoli	1 cup	1.0
Cauliflower	1 cup	1.0
Cabbage	1½ cups	1.0
Spinach	1 cup	0.8
Squash	1 cup	0.9
Green beans	1 cup	0.7

Vegetables	Serving Size	BUs
Brussels sprouts	1 cup	0.8
Roots	1 cup	0.6
Eggplant	1 cup	0.8
Carrots	1 cup	1.4
Celery	3 sticks	0.5
Cucumber	1 medium	0.5
Lettuce	1 regular dinner salad	0.2
Tomato	1 medium	0.5
Potato	1 medium	2.0
Yam	1 medium	3.0
Corn, fresh	1 large ear	2.5
Corn, frozen	1 small ear	1.5
Peas, frozen	⅔ cup	1.0
Avocado	1 large	1.0

Milk Products		
Whole milk	1 cup	1.0
2 percent milk	1 cup	1.0
Chocolate milk	1 cup	2.8
Yogurt, nonfat with fruit	8 oz.	3.9
Yogurt, whole milk plain	1 cup	1.0
Cheese		
cottage	1½ cups	1.0
cheddar	12 oz.	0.2
Muenster	12 oz.	0.2
Monterey Jack	12 oz.	0.2

Soup, Canned		
Chicken noodle	1 cup	1.5
Black bean	1 cup	2.5
Pasta	1 cup	2.0
Lentil	1 cup	2.0
Vegetable beef	1 cup	1.4

Beverages	*Serving Size*	*BUs*
Juice		
apple	8 oz.	2.4
orange	8 oz.	2.2
grapefruit	8 oz.	1.8
Soda		
Coca-Cola	8 oz.	2.3
Sprite	8 oz.	2.2
Tea	8 oz.	0.0
Coffee (without sugar)	1 cup	0.0
Beer (light)	1 cup	1.0
Beer (dark)	1 cup	1.1
Wine	1 cup	0.8
Liquor	4 oz.	0.0
Cocoa, instant	1 packet	2.5

Baby Foods (in jars)		
Green beans	4 oz. (1 jar)	0.3
Chicken and rice	4 oz.	1.0
Pasta primavera	4 oz.	0.8
Carrots	4 oz.	0.6
Fruit cup	4 oz.	1.4

References

Chapter Two

1. Herodotus. *The Histories* (III/2). A new translation by Aubrey de Selincourt. The Penguin Classics, 1954.
2. Savarin, A. B. *Physiologie du gout.* Dtsch. Ausgabe: Bruckmann Querschnitte, Verlg.-Nr. 1152, F. Bruckmann KG, Munchen, 1962.
3. Banting, W. *Letters on Corpulence.* London, Harrison, 1864.
4. Mackarness, R. *Eat Fat and Grow Slim.* Garden City, N.Y.: Doubleday & Co., 1959.
5. Price, W. *Nutrition and Physical Degeneration,* 6th ed. New Canaan, Conn.: Keats Publishing, Inc., 1997.
6. The Weston A. Price Foundation for Wise Traditions in Food, Farming, and the Healing Arts, PMB #106-380, 4200 Wisconsin Avenue NW, Washington, D.C. 20016.
7. Stefansson, V. *The Fat of the Land.* New York: Macmillan Publishing, 1957.
8. Stefansson, V. *Cancer, Disease of Civilization.* New York: Hill & Wang, 1960.
9. Pennington, A. W. *New England J. Med.* 248 (1953): 959.
10. Pennington, A. W. *Am. J. Digest. Dis.* 21 (1954): 69.
11. Pennington, A. W. *Am. J. Digest. Dis.* 21 (1954): 65.
12. Thorpe, G. L. *J. Amer. Med. Assn.* 165 (1957): 1361.
13. Lutz, W. *Leben Ohne Brot.* Planegg: Springer-Verlag, 1967.
14. Yudkin, J. *Sweet and Dangerous.* New York: Van Rees Press, 1972.
15. Tarnower, H., and S. Baker. *The Complete Scarsdale Medical Diet.* Bantam Books, 1995.
16. Sears, B. *Enter the Zone.* Harper Collins, 1995.

17. Eades, M., and M. Eades. *Protein Power.* Bantam Books, 1997.
18. Steward, H. L., M. Bethea, S. Andrews, and L. Balart. *Sugar Busters.* New York: Ballantine Books, 1995.
19. Atkins, R. *Dr. Atkins' Diet Revolution.* New York: David McMay, 1972 (Reissue 1989).
20. Gittleman, A. L. *Eat Fat, Lose Weight.* Keats Publishing, Inc., 1999.
21. Ezrin, C. *Your Fat Can Make You Thin.* Lowell House, 2000.
22. Kwasniewski, J. *Optimal Nutrition.* Warsaw: Wydawnictwo, 1999.
23. Groves, B. *Eat Fat, Get Thin.* London: Vermilion, 2000.

Chapter Three

1. Schole, J. *Theorie der Stoffwechselregulation unter besonderer Berucksichtigung der Regulation des Wachstums.* Berlin and Hamburg: Paul Parey, 1966.
2. Smith, M. A., and F. Lifshitz. "Excess fruit juice consumption as a contributing factor in nonorganic failure to thrive." *Pediatrics* 93, (1994): 438–443.

Chapter Four

1. Major, C. A., M. J. Henry, M. De Veciana, and M. Morgan. "The effects of carbohydrate restriction in patients with diet-controlled gestational diabetes," *Obstet Gynecol* 91 (1998): 600–604.
2. Thomson, J. E., I. N. Scobie, F. Ballantyne, A. Smith, W. G. Manderson, and A. C. MacCuish. "The effect of carbohydrate restriction on lipoprotein abnormalities in maturity-onset diabetes mellitus" *Acta Diabetol Lat* 17 (1980): 33–39.
3. Coulston, A., C. Hollenbeck, A. Swislocki, and G. Reaven. "Persistence of hypertriglyceridemic effect of low-fat, high-carbohydrate diets in NIDDM patients," *Diabetes Care,* 12 (1989): 94–101.
4. Hollenbeck, C., Coulston, A., C., and G. Reaven. "Effects of sucrose on carbohydrate and lipid metabolism in NIDDM patients" *Diabetes Care,* 12 (1989): 62–66; discussion 81–82.
5. Chen, Y., S. Swami, R. Skowronski, A. Coulston, and G. Reaven. "Effect of variations in dietary fat and carbohydrate intake on postprandial lipemia in patients with noninsulindependent diabetes mellitus." *Journal of Clinical Endocrinology Metabolism* 76 (1993): 347–351.

Chapter Five

1. Lawson, L. D. and F. Kummerow. *Lipids* 14 (1979): 501–503.
2. Garg, M. L. *Lipids* 24 (1989): 334–339.

Chapter Six

1. Descartes, René (Translated by Donald A. Cress). *Discourse on the Method of Rightly Conducting One's Reason and of Seeking Truth in the Sciences.* Cambridge, Mass.: Hackett Publishing Company, 1980.
2. Keys, Ancel. *Seven Countries: A Multivariate Analysis of Death and Coronary Heart Disease.* Cambridge, Mass.: Harvard University Press, 1980.
3. Toshima, H., Y. Koga, and H. Blackburn (eds.). *Lessons for Science from the Seven Countries Study.* International Symposium, Fukuoka, Japan: Springer-Verlag, 1994.
4. Miettinen, M., O. Turpeinen, M. Karvonen, R. Elusuo, and E. Paarilainen "Effect of cholesterol lowering diet on mortality from coronary heart disease and other causes" *The Lancet* 11 (1972): 835.
5. American Cancer Society Cancer Prevention Study. *Report of 20 Years of Progress.*
6. Mann, G. V. (ed.). *Coronary Heart Disease: The Dietary Sense and Nonsense.* London, England: Janus Publishing Company, 1993.
7. Mann, G. V. "Diet Heart, End of an Era." *New England Journal of Medicine* 297 (1977): 644.
8. Multiple Risk Factor Intervention Trial Research Group. "Multiple Risk Factor Intervention Trial: Risk factor changes and mortality results." *Journal of the American Medical Association* 248 (1982): 1465–1477.
9. Gordon, T., W. Kannel, W. Castelli, and T. Dawber. *Archives of Internal Medicine* 141 (1981): 1128.
10. American Cancer Society Cancer Prevention Study *Report.*
11. The Lipid Research Clinic Coronary Primary Prevention Trial Results. *Journal of the American Medical Association* 251 (1984): 351.
12. "Toward Healthful Diets." Report to the U.S. Academy of Science, April 28, 1980.
13. Mohler, H. *Die Cholesterin-Neurose.* Otto Salle Vlg. Frankfurt/Main, 1978.

14. Hu, F., M. Stampfer, E. Rimm, J. Manson, A. Ascherio, G. Colditz, B. Rosner, D. Spiegelman, F. Speizer, F. Sacks, C. Hennekens, and W. Willett. "A prospective study of egg consumption and risk of cardiovascular disease in men and women." *Journal of the American Medical Association* 281 (1999): 1387–1394.

15. Hu, F., M. Stampfer, J. Manson, E. Rimm, G. Colditz, B. Rosner, F. Speizer, F. Sacks, C. Hennekens, and W. Willett "Freqeunt nut consumption and risk of coronary heart disease in women: prospective cohort study." *Boston Medical Journal* 317, (1998): 1341–1345.

16. Hu, F., M. Stampfer, J. Manson, E. Rimm, G. Colditz, F. Speizer, C. Hennekens, and W. Willett "Dietary protein and risk of ischemic heart disease in women" *American Journal of Clinical Nutrition* 70 (1999): 221–227.

17. McCully, K. S. *The Homocysteine Revolution*. New Canaan, Conn.: Keats Publishing, Inc. 1997.

18. McCully, K. S. and Martha McCully. *The Heart Revolution*. New York: Harper Collins, 1999.

19. Mann, J., N. Dudman, X. Guo, D. Li, and A. Sinclair, "The effect of the diet on homocysteine in healthy male subjects." *Netherland Journal of Medicine* 52 (suppl), (1998): S10.

20. McCully, K. "Atherosclerosis, serum cholesterol and the homocysteine theory: a study of 194 consecutive autopsies," *American Journal of Medical Science*, 299 (1990): 217–221.

21. Lutz, W., G. Andresen, and E. Buddecke. "Untersuchungen über den Einfluß einer kohlenhydratarmen Langzeitdiät auf die Arteriosklerose des Huhnes." *Zeitschr. f. Ernahrungs-wissensch* 9 (1969): 222.

22. Sallman, H., G. Harisch, and J. Schole. "Uber den Einfluss kohlenhydratarmer Diaten auf die Arteriosklerose des hunes im Langzeitversuch." *Zbl. Vet. Med.* 23 (1976): 635.

23. Pennington, A. W. *Delaware Medical Journal* 23 (1952): 79.

24. Jones, P., A. Pappu, L. Hatcher, Zi-Chi Li, D. R. Illingworth, and W. Connor. "Dietary cholesterol feeding suppresses human cholesterol synthesis measured by deuterium incorporation and urinary mevalonic acid levels." *Arteriosclerosis, Thrombosis and Vascular Biology* 16 (1996): 1222–1228.

25. Lutz, W. "Die Kohlenhydrat-Theorie der Arteriosclerose."
    Wien. Med. Wschr. 19 (1980): 625.
26. Hous, W. H. *Virchows Arch. Ges. Path.* 359 (1973): 1384–1393.
27. Benditt, E. P. "The Origin of Atherosclerosis," *Scientific American* 236
    (1977): 74.
28. Wingen, A. M., C. Fabian-Bach, F. Schaefer, and O. Mehis. "Ran-
    domised multicentre study of a low-protein diet on the progression of
    chronic renal failure in children," *The Lancet,* 349 (1997): 1117–1123.

Chapter Seven
    1. Crohn, B., B. Ginzburg, and G. Oppenheimer. *Journal of the Ameri-
       can Medical Association* 99 (1932): 1323.
    2. Thornton, J., et al. "Diet and Crohn's Disease, Characteristics of the
       Pre-Illness Diet." *British Medical Journal* 365 (1979): 74.
    3. Brandes, J. "Zuckerfreie Diät als Langzeit-bzw. Intervall-Behandlung
       in der Remissionsphase des Morbus Crohn eine prospektive Studie."
       Leber, Magen,Darm 12 (1982): 225.
    4. Lutz, W. "Morbus Crohn unter kohlenhydratarmer Kost." *Munchner.
       Med. Wochenschrift* 50 (1987): 921–923.
    5. Lorenz-Meyer, H., P. Bauer, et al. *Scandanavian Journal of Gastroen-
       terology* 31, (1996): 778.
    6. Lutz, W. *Wien. Med. Wschr.* (1965): 516.
    7. Lutz, W. *Monatskurse f. ärztl. Fortbildung* 18 (1968): 615.
    8. Lutz, W. "Die Behandlung der Colitis ulcerosa durch Kohlenhy-
       dratebe-schrdnkung, Bericht fiber 40 Fdlle." *Wien. Med. Wschr.* 25/26
       (1967): 660.
    9. Lutz, W. "Kohlenhydratarme Diät bei Colitis ulcerosa" *Münch. Med.
       Wschr.* 28 (1979): 953.
   10. Lutz, W. "Kohlenhydratarme Diqt bei Colitis ulcerosa und Morbus
       Crohn." *Coloproctology* 3 (1981): 349.

Chapter Eight
    1. Mackarness, R. *Eat Fat and Grow Slim.* Garden City, N.Y.: Doubleday
       & Co., 1959.
    2. Fredericks, C. *Low Carbohydrate Diet.* New York: Award Books, 1965.
    3. Yudkin, J. *This Slimming Business.* London: McGibbon & Kee, 1958.

4. Taller, H. *Calories Don't Count.* New York: Simon & Schuster, 1961.
5. Atkins, R. *Dr. Atkins' Diet Revolution.* New York: David McMay, 1972.
6. Jameson, G. and E. Williams. *The Drinking Man's Diet.* San Francisco: Cameron & Co., 1965.
7. Carise, E. *Punkt-Diät* Editions Indigo Etablissements. Vaduz, 5.-6. Auflage (1968).
8. Lutz, W. "Das endocrine Syndrom des adipösen jugendlichen" *Wien. Med. Wschr.* (1964): 451.

Chapter Nine
1. U.S. Department of Agriculture, *The Yearbook of Agriculture.* 1959.
2. Allan, C. B., G. Lacourciere, and T. C. Stadtman. "Responsiveness of Selenoproteins to Dietary Selenium." *Annual Reviews of Nutrition* 19 (1999): 1–16.
3. Gorlatov, S. N., and T. C. Stadtman. "Human thioredoxin reductase from HeLa cells: Selective alkylation of selenocysteine in the protein inhibits enzyme activity and reduction with NADPH influences affinity to heparin" *Proceedings of the National Acadamy of Sciences* USA 95 (1998): 8520–8525.
4. Sinatra, S. *L-carnitine and the Heart.* New Canaan, Conn.: Keats Publishing, 1999.
5. Kelly, G. "L-carnitine: Therapeutic applications of a conditionally essential amino acid" *Alter Med Review* 3, (1998): 345–360.
6. Singh, R., M. Niaz, P. Agarwal, R. Beegum, S. Rastogi, and D. Sachan, "A randomised, double-blind, placebo-controlled trial of L-carnitine in suspected acute myocardial infarction" *Postgrad. Med. J* 72 (1996): 45–50.
7. Mingrove, G., A. Greco, et al. "L-carnitine improves glucose disposal in type 2 diabetic patients." *J. Am. Coll. Nutr.* 18 (1999): 77–82.
8. Sinatra, S. "Care, cancer and coenzyme Q10." *J. Am. Coll. Cardiol.* 33 (1999): 897–899.

Chapter Ten
1. Watson, J., and F. Crick. "Genetical implications of the structure of deoxyribonucleic acid." *Nature* 171 (1953): 964–967.
2. Warburg, O. "On the origin of cancer cells." *Science,* 123 (1956): 309–317.

3. Abercrombie, M., and J. Heaysman. *Nature* 174 (1954): 697.

4. Pederson, P. "Tumor mitochondria and the bioenergetics of cancer cells." *Progress in Experimental Tumor Research* 22 (1978): 190–274.

5. Gauthier, T., C. Denis-Pouxviel, and J. Murat. "Respiration of mitochondria isolated from differentiated and undifferentiated HT29 colon cancer cells in the presence of various substrates and ADP generating systems." *International Journal of Biochemistry* 22 (1990): 411–417.

6. Dunn, S., F. Kari, J. French, J. Leininger, G. Travlos, R. Wilson, and J. C. Barrett. "Dietary restriction reduces insulin-like growth factor 1 levels, which modulates apoptosis, cell proliferation, and tumor progression in p53-deficient mice." *Cancer Research*, 57 (1997): 4667–4672.

7. Snyder, D., D. Clemmons, and L. Underwood. "Dietary carbohydrate content determines responsiveness to growth hormone in energy-restricted humans." *Journal of Clinical Endocrynology and Metabolism*, 69 (1989): 745–752.

8. Caufriez, A., J. Golstein, P. Lebrun, A. Herchuelz, R. Furlanetto, and G. Copinschi. "Relationships between immunoreactive somatomedin-C, insulin and T$_3$ patterns during fasting in obese subjects." *Clinical Endocrinology*. 20 (1984): 65–70.

9. Hankinson, S., W. Willett, G. Colditz, et al. "Circulating concentrations of insulin-like growth factor-1 and risk of breast cancer," *The Lancet*, 351 (1998): 1393–1396.

10. Holmes, M., D. Hunter, G. Colditz. "Association of diatary intake of fat and fatty acids with risk of breast cancer." *Journal of the American Medical Association*. 281 (1999): 914–920.

11. Gertig, D., S. Hankinson, H. Hough, et al. "N-acetyl transferase 2 genotypes, meat intake and breast cancer risk." *International Journal of Cancer* 80 (1999): 13–17.

12. Holmes, M., M. Stampfer, G. Colditz, B. Rosner, D. Hunter, and W. Willett. "Dietary factors and the survival of women with breast carcinoma." *Cancer* 86 (1999): 826–835.

13. Hankinson, S., W. Willett, J. Manson, et al. "Plasma sex steroid hormone levels and risk of breast cancer in postmenopausal women," *Journal of the National Cancer Institute* 90 (1998): 1292–1299.

14. Lutz, W., and H. Iselstöger. *Munch. Med. Wschr.* 102 (1960): 1963.

15. Fuchs, C., E. Giovannucci, G. Colditz, et al. "Dietary fiber and the risk of colorectal cancer and adenoma in women" *New England Journal of Medicine* 340 (1999): 169–176.

16. Muir, J., K. Walker, M. Kaimakamis, et al. "Modulation of fecal markers relevant to colon cancer risk: A high-starch Chinese diet did not generate expected beneficial changes relative to a western-type diet," *American Journal of Clinical Nutrition* 68 (1998): 372–379.

Chapter Eleven

1. Stanford, C. *The Hunting Apes.* Princeton: Princeton University Press, 1999.

2. Harris, M. *Cannibals and Kings.* New York: Random House Inc., 1977.

3. Angel, L. "Paleoecology, Paleodemography, and Health" In Polgar (ed.) (1975): 167–190.

4. Lutz, W. "The Colonization of Europe and Our Western Diseases," *Medical Hypothesis* 45 (1995): 115–120.

5. U.S. Centers for Disease Control and Prevention and World Health Organization.

6. Green, A., E. Galke, and C. Patterson. "The Eurodiabetic ACE Study." *The Lancet* 339 (1992): 905–909.

7. Kurtzke, J. *Clinical Microbiology Reviews* (1993): 382–427.

Chapter Twelve

1. Fallon, S. *Nourishing Traditions.* Washington, D.C.: New Trends Publishing Inc., 1999.

Index